TREADMILL
TO
OBLIVION

TREADMILL
TO
OBLIVION

by

Fred Allen

WITH DRAWINGS BY HIRSCHFELD

An Atlantic Monthly Press Book

Boston . Little, Brown and Company . *Toronto*

LIBRARY OF CONGRESS CATALOG CARD NO. 54–11132

Published November 1954
Reprinted November 1954 (four times)
Reprinted December 1954

PN 1991.4

A42

ATLANTIC–LITTLE, BROWN BOOKS
ARE PUBLISHED BY
LITTLE, BROWN AND COMPANY
IN ASSOCIATION WITH
THE ATLANTIC MONTHLY PRESS

Published simultaneously in Canada
by Little, Brown & Company (Canada) Limited

PRINTED IN THE UNITED STATES OF AMERICA

TO PORTLAND

Who *stayed in a closet* **until**
I *finished writing this book*

Ed O'Connor, who has the memory
of an elephant, helped me with this tome.
Ted Weeks, who has the energy
of a beaver, also helped.
It proves that with an elephant's memory,
a beaver's energy and two friends,
a radio actor can write a book.

Contents

PART I

In the Beginning

In the spring of 1932, I had finished a two-year run in *Three's A Crowd,* a musical revue in which I appeared with Clifton Webb and Libby Holman. The following September I was to go into a new show. I had no contract; merely the producer's promise. When I returned to New York to start rehearsals, I discovered that there was to be no show. It had been a hot summer. Many people hadn't been able to keep things. One of the things the producer hadn't been able to keep was his promise. With the advance of refrigeration, I hope that along with the frozen foods someday we will have frozen conversation. A person will be able to keep a frozen promise indefinitely. This will be a boon to show business where more chorus girls are kept than promises.

With no immediate plans for the theater, I began to wonder about radio. Many of the big-name comedians were appearing on regular programs. In the theater the actor had uncertainty, broken promises, constant travel and a gypsy existence. In radio, if you were successful, there was an assured season of work. The show could not close if there was nobody in the balcony. There was no travel and the actor could enjoy a permanent home. There may have been other advantages but I didn't need to know them.

The pioneer comedians on radio were Amos and Andy, Ray Knight and his Cuckoo Hour, the Gold Dust Twins, Stoopnagle and Budd and the Tasty Yeast Jesters. With the exception of Amos and Andy, who had been playing smalltime vaudeville theaters under the name of Sam and Henry, the others were trained and developed in radio. All of these artists performed their comedy routines in studios without audiences. Their entertainment was planned for the listener at home.

In the early 1930's when the Broadway comedians descended on radio, things went from hush to raucous. The theater buffoon had no conception of the medium and no time to study its requirements. The Broadway slogan was "It's dough — let's go!" Eddie Cantor, Jack Pearl, Ed Wynn, Joe Penner and others were radio sensations. They brought their audiences into the studios, used their theater techniques and their old vaudeville jokes, and laughter, rehearsed or spontaneous, started exploding between the commercials. The cause of this merriment was not always clear. The bewildered set owner in Galesburg, Illinois, suddenly realized that he no longer had to be able to understand radio comedy. As he sat in his Galesburg living room he knew that he had proxy audiences sitting in radio studios in New York, Chicago and Hollywood watching the comedians, laughing and shrieking "Vass you dere, Charlie" and "Wanna buy a duck" for him.

The big comedians felt that if they entertained the studio audiences their radio success was assured. Eddie Cantor wore funny costumes, pummeled his announcer with his fist and frequently kicked his guest star to obtain results. A Cantor show would open with the announcer shouting "And here

[4]

comes Eddie! Eddie's wearing fifty balloons tied to his coat! Ha! ha! Eddie hopes he'll get a break tonight. Ha! ha!" (*Applause and whistling.*) Ed Wynn made complete changes of funny hats and grotesque coats between comedy joke routines. Other popular comedians threw pies and squirted seltzer at their stooges.

Analyzing the comedian's problem in this new business, it seemed to me that the bizarre-garbed, joke-telling funster was ogling extinction. The monotony of his weekly recital of unrelated jokes would soon drive listeners to other diversions. Since the radio comedian really had to depend on the ears of the home audience for his purpose, I thought that a complete story told each week or a series of episodes and comedy situations might be a welcome change. It would enable the listener to flex his imagination, and perhaps make him want to follow the experiences of the characters involved. This, if it worked, would insure the radio comedian a longer life. Hoping for longevity in the new medium, I planned a series of programs using a different business background each week — a newspaper office, a department store, a bank, a detective agency, etc. The comedy would involve the characters employed in, or indigenous to, the assorted locales.

An audition program was prepared, a cast assembled and rehearsals started. Now that I had a radio program, all I needed was a sponsor. My agent heard, via the grapevine (in those days he had to hear everything via the grapevine: he had no telephone), that Linit was looking for a new show. Linit was a beauty powder made by the Corn Products Company. The president of Corn Products was a very busy man. He used radio extensively to advertise his many products but he had scant time to bother with the content of his programs. My agent wondered how we could ever catch him for an audition.

There was a story told about this gentleman. It seems that he had engaged a singer called Lazy Dan. When Lazy Dan's show went on at 7.30 P.M. the president, who rushed from the office to his speedboat every night, said, "Why do they put Lazy Dan on so early? Why don't they put him on at 9:30 at night when people are eating their dinners?" For months Lazy Dan sang his songs every night at 7:30; for months the president scurried from the office to his boat, sped home and had his dinner at 9:30. One night there was a severe storm. The president could not use his boat. He had to stay in the city. He remembered about Lazy Dan. That night he heard the show. The next day Lazy Dan was fired.

It developed that the president of Corn Products was so busy that he could not come to the studio to see an audition of our new show. He could not hold up his bustling routine to listen over a special wire. He suggested that we send someone to his office with a portable phonograph and a recording of the audition. The show could be played in his hectic presence and he would listen as best he could.

My agent was galvanized into action. He borrowed a portable phonograph, tucked the record under his arm, and started downtown in the subway to the Corn Products building. Upon his arrival my agent was ushered into the presence of the whirling tycoon. He fumbled nervously as he tried to start the machine. The phonograph had been jarred in the subway. The mechanism refused to cooperate. The record

[6]

would spin, the musical overture play, but after a few lines of my opening scene the record would stop abruptly. This sampling was repeated several times. My agent was a wreck. The president was trying to subdue his temper. The next time the record stopped the president exploded. "That's enough," he roared. "Never mind the show. Get me that man with the flat voice!"

I was the man with the flat voice. I was in radio. We had a contract for thirteen weeks. I say "we" advisedly. According to the fine print, my agent and I were to supply a weekly radio program, to pay actors, writers, guests, a director and any other essentials we required for $1000 per week. My agent went right to work. He borrowed $100 from me. My agent always liked to have his commission in advance. It not only gave him a sense of security, it protected him from possible calamitous developments.

My agent's next move was to escort me into the presence of the head of the advertising agency that handled the Linit account. This gentleman happened to be married to the daughter of one of the important men in the Corn Products Company. Thus he was qualified to be an authority on advertising, comedy and things in general. The head man shook my hand with a *rigor mortis* grip. I was quickly scrutinized and totaled. I sensed that I didn't amount to much. The head man told me that he had seen me in the theater but he didn't know about my radio potential. "Who will write the programs?" he said. "I will," I answered. "Okay," he shot back, "write a program and bring it up here next week." I went home and went to work.

[7]

On the appointed day I returned with a completed script. I was ushered into the conference room. After I had been allowed to sit there long enough to be impressed, the door flew open, the head of the agency stepped in briskly. He was followed by two echo men. Echo men are very important in the world of advertising. They are men who follow in the wake of the big executive and echo his sentiments as they are expressed. One of the echo men wore a pince-nez that seemed to be too tight. It bunched up the skin at the top of his nose. I will never forget this character. As I took the script from my briefcase to read it, the head man plucked the script from my hand and turned it over to the pince-nez chap. Pince-Nez proceeded to read my comedy script. It was obvious that he had no sense of humor. In a dull dreary voice he read through joke after joke, and page after page. He sounded like a mortician taking inventory. When he had finished, and had pinched his pince-nez to let the skin at the top of his nose unbunch for a second, he handed the script back to me. Nobody had laughed. Nobody had smiled. The three men just sat there staring at me. I felt small enough to crawl into my briefcase. I thought about it but realized that once inside the briefcase I couldn't close the zipper and disappear completely from view.

As I stood up and prepared to leave through the keyhole, the head of the agency said, "Are you going to bring another show next week?" I didn't know whether he was inviting me or daring me to return. I took a chance. "Yes, sir," I replied. The next two weeks I wrote shows and each week brought one to the agency. The head and the echo men assembled. Pince-

Nez read the script with his funereal touch. For three weeks, during the script readings, the virgin calm of the conference room had never once been violated by an audible titter or chuckle.

The third reading was the last. The contract starting date had arrived and on Sunday, October 23, 1932, the Linit show finally got out of the conference room and made its debut over the Columbia Broadcasting System.

One of our early Linit programs was called the Side Show, a Circus Episode. This short section of the script reads like museum fun today. But circa 1932 it assumed the guise of comedy dialogue:

Linit Bath Club Revue

ALLEN   Good evening, ladies and gentlemen. Tonight the Linit Bath Club Revue takes you behind the scenes at the Side Show. I shall be the barker, and while I'm teasing the Wild Man to make him good and wild for you tonight, the Gold Medal Band will play something brassy for your entertainment.

ORCHESTRA   *(Circus Music)*

ALLEN   Now if you'll just step a little closer, folks. . . . Move right up to the platform please. You're about to see the greatest free show ever presented with a traveling organization of this sort. On the inside you will see the Carnival of Freaks: Jolly Emma, the Fat Girl. . . . Scrawny Ralph, the

[9]

Living Skeleton: he rattles when he walks. . . .
Handy Roger, the Armless Wonder: shaves himself, plays the ukelele, and does card tricks. He's wonderful, he's marvelous, the only armless sculptor in the world!

VOICE It's a swindle!

ALLEN What's that, neighbor?

VOICE How can a guy with no arms be a sculptor?

ALLEN I'll tell you how, friend: Handy Roger puts the chisel in his mouth and his wife hits him on the back of the head with a mallet. And he's only one of the many wonders you'll see on the inside. There's Leo, the Dog-faced Boy! Daredevil Ginsberg, the Human Rocket! And, as an extra added attraction, the person holding the lucky number at this performance will receive a psychic reading free of charge. All for only ten cents, folks!

VOICE What about the free show?

ALLEN I heard that, friend. It's just about to start, and the first artist you see . . . FREE . . . GRATIS . . . AND FOR NOTHING . . . is Gulpo, the Sword Swallower! Professor Gulpo, Ladies and Gentlemen, swallows anything from his pride to a lightning rod. Introducing . . . Professor Gulpo!

GULPO (With dialect) My first experiment: swallowing watch and chain!

ALLEN It's remarkable! Stupendous! Hold the baby up, lady: this is a demonstration every child should see. Okay, Professor!

[10]

GULPO   UGH. . . . UGH. *(Grunts as though removing watch, band strikes chord)* I thank you. And now I swallow ordinary umbrella!

ALLEN   Watch him closely! There it goes: the professor is putting something away for a rainy day. There you are folks! And now the professor will remove the umbrella!

ORCHESTRA   *(Drum roll)*

GULPO   UGH. . . . HELP. . . . OH . . . UGH. . . . HELP!

ALLEN   Shake a tonsil, Gulpo. Is anything wrong?

GULPO   It's stuck! *(Groans)*

ALLEN   Why didn't you say so? Excuse me, folks. Sometimes the professor's stomach snaps at something he's swallowed and we have a little trouble. Let me get the handle.

GULPO   OH. . . . OH. . . . You're killing me!

ALLEN   It won't come out, Gulpo. I pulled something. It opened the umbrella. I guess one of the ribs is caught on your spine. You ought to do this trick with a cane.

VOICES   Take him off! He's terrible! Go on with the show!

ALLEN   You'd better beat it, Professor. They're getting noisy.

GULPO   Ugh. . . . Take bow.

ALLEN   You can't take a bow with that umbrella in you. When you stoop over the end will come through your back and tear your coat to pieces. Just wave your hand. They'll know you're through; they knew it ten minutes ago.

After the first few programs, I realized that a person who attempted to write a half-hour comedy show week after week had to end up talking to himself. And a comedian who starts talking to himself becomes his own audience. This is fatal. I was not only writing the entire program, I was eternally rewriting it, rehearsing it and appearing on it. The day after each show I had to attend a meeting at which a transcription of the program was played. Pince-Nez and the other boys regaled me with their post-mortems. They commented on the comedy, the singing, the music and the sound effects. The show had been done. It was like trying to breathe yesterday's air.

With all of this going on I knew I would soon need a psychiatrist or somebody who could help me. Radio was new. It hadn't developed any comedy writers. David Freedman, who was writing the Eddie Cantor program, Billy Wells, writing Jack Pearl's Baron Munchausen routines, Harry Conn, Jack Benny's first writer, and the few others were high-priced revue and vaudeville writers. They were enticed into radio with bonanza salaries and I suspect that each of them was earning more than the $1000 we had available for our entire show.

Before I had time to look around to make sure that my quandary was gaining on me, a friend told me about a fledgling critic, working on the *Motion Picture Herald,* who was planning to take up radio writing. The critic's name was Harry Tugend. We met, discussed the problems, and agreed that they were insurmountable. Harry was engaged and for four years Harry and I wrote the programs and coped with the forces that attempted to impede our weekly trek from the

[12]

writing session to the microphone. Harry graduated from radio and went to Hollywood, where he has been a very successful writer and producer for many years. I may end up working for Harry someday.

About this time the sponsors of radio programs suddenly found themselves floundering around in show business. Men who ran oil companies, drug, food and tobacco corporations, were attending auditions, engaging talent and in too many instances their untutored opinions adversely influenced the destinies of artists, singers and musicians.

When Ed Wynn was being considered for radio he was starring on Broadway in his own show, *The Laugh Parade*. To make sure that Ed, who had been a star in the theater practically all of his life, would be suitable for the Texaco Star Theater radio program, a group of the Texas Company officials decided to attend Ed's show. To double-check on how Ed would come over the air, the oil company executives sat through Ed Wynn's entire show with their eyes closed. *P.S.:* When they opened their eyes Ed got the job.

Ed Wynn, as the Fire Chief, was one of radio's first big stars. Ed was also one of the first comedians to insist on an audience in the studio to react to his jokes. In the radio studio, atop the New Amsterdam Theater which had formerly been the Ziegfeld Roof, the broadcasting company had hung a glass curtain that separated the audience from the actors. The purpose of the curtain was to eliminate any audience reaction or noise that might be picked up by the microphones and go out over the air. Before Ed Wynn started to broadcast from this studio, he insisted that the glass curtain be raised so that the laughter and applause that accompanied his jokes could get out over the air. Ed has a lot to answer for.

It was inevitable that the sponsors would soon consider themselves authorities on the tastes and entertainment preferences of the general public. One successful tobacco man had a popular dance band on the air. The day of the show, the band leader had to list on a blackboard all of the musical numbers he intended to play. At rehearsal time the tobacco man and his wife arrived at the studio. As the band played, the tobacco man and his wife danced. Any number to which they couldn't enjoy dancing had to be rubbed off the blackboard and another number substituted for the show.

On our first show the pince-nez gentleman wanted me to dress up for the broadcast as a Keystone Cop. His idea was to have me stand at the studio door, brandishing a stuffed club, and as the audience filed in hit each person over the head. I asked Pince-Nez what purpose this would serve. He said, "The audience will know you're the comedian."

In the process of imposing their personal likes on the radio listener, many sponsors were influenced by the opinions of their friends, their relatives and their wives. Our busy employer apparently listened to his wife. After we had done a few shows we were advised that the sponsor's wife liked organ music. Our musical conductor, Lou Katzman (I hope you won't think I am a name-dropper), was ordered to add an organ solo to the program. It was to be played in the middle of the performance. Playing an organ solo midway through a comedy show is like planting a pickle in the center of a charlotte russe. I remember one of our programs, the Return of Admiral Byrd. It was a satirical account of the Admiral packing to leave the Pole. After the Admiral had finished tidying up his igloo, and was busy bidding farewell to his many penguin friends, suddenly we had to stop, let the Admiral pull up a frozen hummock and sit down, until our organ interlude was concluded.

Later, the sponsor's wife learned that the organ was not being played in our studio but was actually two miles away in another studio. She was eager to share her amazement with the audience, so we were compelled to add this announcement to our text:

ANNOUNCER   Ladies and gentlemen, before returning you to Fred Allen's "Linit Show" we will synchronize the Wurlitzer Organ Music by Ann Leaf with the music of Lou Katzman's Orchestra here in the studio. Ann Leaf is seated in the Paramount Studio, two miles from the orchestra. The selection to be played is "Beautiful Love."

A regular feature of our Linit program was the sequence with Portland. No one has ever asked me how we acquired this entertaining cameo. One day I am sure some busybody is going to bring this up. I will be ready with this explanation.

Portland and I started doing a vaudeville act together shortly after we were married. In vaudeville, when a comedian married he immediately put his wife in the act. The wife didn't have to have any talent. It was economic strategy. With a double act the comedian could get a salary increase from the booking office. The additional money would pay for his wife's wardrobe, her railroad fares and the extra hotel expenses. In vaudeville, the actor roamed the country and the upkeep on a nonworking wife was an important item. Having his wife in his act enabled the comedian to know where she was all the time. This made it possible for him to concentrate on his comedy.

Portland and I were married in May. During the summer I wrote an act for us. On Labor Day, a day that glorifies work, Portland, in the great vaudeville tradition, started to work in the act. Later in the season we played the Palace. (I merely mention the Palace to prove that we had a good act.) Portland and I (that wasn't our billing: it wasn't "I and Portland" either) appeared in all the leading vaudeville theaters from coast to coast. Later, we were in two successful Broadway revues, *The Little Show* and *Three's A Crowd*.

When radio became a challenge we accepted it. We were married until death do us part and radio sure wasn't going to interfere with this arrangement. Radio might hasten it but not otherwise thwart the overall deal. Our first concern was to create a character that the listener at home would associate with Portland's voice. That was our problem. Over the microphone, Portland's voice sounded like two slate pencils mating or a clarinet reed calling for help. I still don't know whether it was the microphone that distorted Portland's natural voice or whether an element of nervousness was involved. When Portland writes her book, she may divulge.

Most of the other radio couples — Burns and Allen, the Easy Aces, Fibber McGee and Molly and Ozzie and Harriet, to name a few — used their marital status and their domestic experiences for comedy purposes. They played themselves and their programs were almost weekly diaries that proved that they faced the same dilemmas that the average middle-class couple found confronting them in their daily lives.

Jack Benny and Mary Livingston were the exception. No mention was ever made in their dialogue that they were married. Mary's comedy was derived from reading frequent letters from home, criticizing Jack and his activities, falling in love with good-looking male guest stars on the program and engaging in assorted sophisticated peccadillos.

Portland didn't seem to fit into any of the accepted categories. The more we heard her radio voice, the more we realized that a character, a small E-flat Frankenstein monster, would have to be custom-made for her. And so she came out a subnormal adolescent who talked in tones you had to associate with Portland. These conversational sounds could come from no other source.

When the show was new, Portland's routines usually came out something like this:

SECRETARY   There's a little girl waiting outside.
ALLEN   Let her age awhile and send her in.
PORTLAND   Hello.
ALLEN   Oh, hello, Portland. What are you doing here in New York?
PORTLAND   I come every year to go to the aquarium.
ALLEN   On a pleasure trip?
PORTLAND   I have to go on business.

[17]

ALLEN   Nobody has any business in the aquarium. People only go in there to get out of the rain.

PORTLAND   You're thinking of museums.

ALLEN   Maybe you're right. But what do you do in the aquarium?

PORTLAND   Papa sends our goldfish there. I throw them in the tank.

ALLEN   What for?

PORTLAND   He says the goldfish get dizzy at home, swimming around in a little globe all year.

ALLEN   So he gives them an outing every winter, is that it?

PORTLAND   Yes. I bring them down to the aquarium for two weeks.

ALLEN   Does it do them any good?

PORTLAND   I guess it helps them socially. They get to meet a lot of nice fish.

ALLEN   Have you ever lost any goldfish?

PORTLAND   Yes, one year my uncle brought them down.

ALLEN   What happened then?

PORTLAND   Everything was all right until he went to get the fish to take them home.

ALLEN   Couldn't he catch them?

PORTLAND   No. My uncle fell in the tank and they couldn't tell him from the other poor fish.

ALLEN   What did they do?

PORTLAND   They threw a picture of my aunt in the water. And when one of the fish saw it and tried to get out of the water, they caught him.

[18]

ALLEN   And that was . . .
PORTLAND   My uncle.

After a twenty-six-week season, the Linit show left the air. Mothballs were put on the organ and we removed our stooges from the premises. Harry Tugend and I had written the entire series together. We were learning about radio and experimenting with a variety of comedy characters and situations. The joke-telling comedians were still more popular but our shows were improving. They had pace and were acquiring an assembly-line polish. The most encouraging progress we had made, however, was the survey figures which showed the industry that our program's rating had finally gotten off the ground.

One day, as I was busy being unemployed, my agent called. Controlling his excitement he informed me that the partner in one of the biggest advertising agencies in town wanted to see me. It was urgent. I had heard of this man. There was a rumor that he was so big he had a wastebasket in his office in which he threw people. When I arrived breathlessly at the sanctum of the Madison Avenue messiah, before I was all the way through the door, he came to the point. He needed my advice. I had never seen this man before and he needed my advice. I guess that's the way things go in the advertising game. The partner of a great company often needs advice from an actor who is unemployed. Even before I could get my hat off I learned that he was in trouble. It seems that he had imitated our Linit show format, had engaged another comedian and was presenting this duplicate program on another network for Hellmann's Mayonnaise. His carbon show was a disappointment. In a capsule that was his trouble. The memo merchant had summoned me to explain why the imitation was not getting the same results we had gotten. He told me that he had been seriously worried when he called me but since then he had had the good luck to engage Norman Anthony, the editor of *Ballyhoo*. *Ballyhoo* was a humor and cartoon magazine that specialized in lampooning big business and advertising. It was currently convulsing the country. The advertising giant was convinced that Mr. Anthony was the answer to his prayer. Mr. Anthony could supply the elements that were lacking. The man of industry thanked me profusely for my needless visit. As I started to congratulate him on having solved his problem, a secretary appeared, and the next thing I knew I was out in the hall.

Shaken by this experience, I left for Maine to start an early vacation. One morning, about two weeks later, as Portland was preparing a typical Maine breakfast, poached egg on raw lobster, there was a tumult at the front of the cottage. I opened the door to find a native puffing profusely. Obviously he had been running. When he was able to get his breath he panted, "Come quick, Mr. Allen! Yer wanted onto the tellyfun, it's New York City a-callin'! Foller me." I grabbed my windbreaker. After I had "follered" him for about a mile down the road the native stopped, pointed to the edge of a forest and announced, "Thar she be!" Sure enough, nailed to the trunk of one of the trees there was a small wooden box. Through the partly open door of the box I saw a telephone. I still don't know what that telephone was doing hanging on a tree. The tree might have been an old telephone pole that had bloomed again.

I picked up the receiver. It was my advertising friend. He was in trouble once more. Hellmann's Mayonnaise was dissatisfied with the program and was threatening to cancel. There was a crisis. (Crisis is a word used in advertising circles to refer to any minor incident to which the word "emergency" cannot be applied.) The crisis, in this case, could only be averted if I would come back to New York and take over the show!

This led to our next radio venture, the Salad Bowl Revue, which was sponsored by the Hellmann's Mayonnaise Company. Mayonnaise is a seasonal product and every year the Hellmann people confined their radio campaign to the summer months when salads were popular. After the spurious version, apparently our conception of our own show met with the sponsor's approval. When October 1 arrived, the date that the mayonnaise advertising was normally discontinued, the Hellmann Company announced that it was keeping the program on until January 1. Long after lettuce, endive, romaine and other leafy salad ingredients had disappeared that fall, our announcer carried on extolling the merits and the qualities of Hellmann's Mayonnaise. I often wondered about the housewives who had no sales resistance that winter. What were they eating under their Hellmann's Mayonnaise?

During the Salad Bowl series we introduced a feature we called the Etiquette Department. We encouraged listeners who had etiquette problems to send them in to us and we would cope with them over the air. We were not interested in encouraging gentility in middle-class families; we were merely trying to stimulate the program's mail. In those days mail was very important. A comedian's fan-mail was checked regularly by the network, the advertising agency and the sponsor's office; and in these quarters the popularity of the program was determined by the quantity and the content of the mail. The response to our etiquette offer was no deluge. At its peak it attained trickle proportions. Either the listeners didn't know what etiquette was or they were able to handle their own problems. This forced us to invent most of our questions. After a few weeks we were commenting on manners and decorum, taking etiquette for a ride and leaving Emily at the post.

The etiquette problems were unusual. These are two exhibits:

ALLEN   Well, our Etiquette Department is hitting on all one, ladies and gentlemen, and our postcard tonight comes from Joseph Keesey, of Columbia, Pennsylvania. Mr. Keesey says, "Whenever I eat corn on the cob my derby works down over my eyes and I can't see what I'm doing. I have bitten one thumb half off and I'll have to give up the corn or both of my thumbs."

A derby is never worn at the dinner table during the summer, Mr. Keesey. The well-dressed man wears a straw hat or a beret in the dining room.

If you too are bothered by some problem in etiquette, ladies and gentlemen, why not send me your dilemma on a postcard. Send it in care of this station, and I shall be happy to help you as I have helped Mr. Keesey.

ALLEN Our postcard tonight comes from Mr. John W. Dunn of Cape Elizabeth, Maine. He says, "A friend of mine has been in the hospital for the past two weeks. I have bought him some fruit — a dozen bananas, to be exact — but I haven't had time to get down to the hospital to eat the fruit at my friend's bedside. The bananas are turning black. What should I do?"

It is perfectly permissible, Mr. Dunn, to eat the fruit at home. You can mail the banana skins to your friend in the hospital to prove you have been thinking of him. I know he will understand. You might mail your friend's nurse a wastebasket, too, so that she will have some place to throw the banana skins when they arrive.

We were constantly making minor changes in the program content. To give us greater scope for comedy subject matter, we later abandoned the Etiquette Department and started the Question Box. We were now able to advise the listener on any subject he could get by the censor. We were giving health precautions, hints on clothing styles, publicizing little-known inventions, etc. Two of the inventions we called to America's attention were the permanent wet lapel, to enable floorwalkers to keep their gardenias fresh through the entire working day, and the perfumed bookmark. If you couldn't find your bookmark you smelled along the end of the pages until you located it. With the Question Box and the comedy routines we added sketches and topical burlesques to climax the half hour.

Around the end of December, that year, the Hellmann Company realized that there was nothing to put their mayonnaise on but the actors, and we severed our pleasant relations with this friendly corporation.

We had still been working for the same advertising agency, one of whose partners had originally helped himself to our program format. With the termination of our Salad Bowl Revue contract, I was again called into the presence of the happy huckster. I thought that perhaps he was in trouble again and that he was bringing Norman Anthony in to replace me. I was wrong. This time he had news of a new sponsor. Sal Hepatica was going on the air. Sal Hepatica knew no season. As soon as Harry and I could get a show together we were all back at the microphones with a new program, the Sal Hepatica Revue. I remember our first performance. The show started. The announcer shouted "Sal Hepatica is on the air!" The orchestra played "In Your Easter Bonnet . . ."

PART II
Town Hall Tonight

The Sal Hepatica Revue had been running along smoothly for almost three months when again I was called to heel by the head of the agency. Advertising agencies always confuse me. I suspect that many of them confuse themselves. To me, an advertising agency is 85 per cent confusion and 15 per cent commission. A vice-president in an advertising agency is a "molehill man." A molehill man is a pseudo-busy executive who comes to work at 9 A.M. and finds a molehill on his desk. He has until 5 P.M. to make this molehill into a mountain. An accomplished molehill man will often have his mountain finished even before lunch.

The head of our agency was a very successful man in his field. He would enjoy being in any field. He suffered from claustrophobia. He had to stay out of Rhode Island. He always felt that the state was closing in on him. He was the prolific father of many innovations in the advertising world. (The advertising world had space men in it before space men were in science fiction.) He inaugurated the practise of office-testing products. When the agency obtained a new advertising account, all of the employees had to try the product immediately and report their reactions and any comment they had to make. For example, if it was a new soap account the girls and the boys working in the agency took a sample cake of the soap and tried it at home. They checked on the soap's aroma, lather potential and its cleansing properties and turned in a detailed report on their findings. A new headache tablet would be distributed to the staff and probably be very welcome. In the advertising game (it isn't a business) a headache is an occupational side effect. The new headache tablet would be tested and a written report turned in. I never knew what happened to the staff the day the agency took over the Sal Hepatica account.

When I made my appearance in the upholstered oven in which the head man made his daily bread (and an occasional decision), I discovered that there was more executive skullduggery afoot. Another radio program was going to be pilfered. Fortunately, this time it was not our show. The Bristol-Myers Company had a contract with the radio network for an hour of time on Wednesday nights. From 9 to 9.30 P.M. the company had a musical program advertising Ipana Toothpaste, one of its products. From 9.30 to 10 P.M. they sponsored our show for Sal Hepatica.

The interoffice knavery was to convince Bristol-Myers that, since our Sal Hepatica program was attracting a much larger audience than their Ipana charade, we should filch the Ipana thirty minutes from a competing advertising agency, take over the entire sixty minutes and create a new hour show advertising both products. Eyes were raised in conference — advertising two products on one radio program was tampering with precedent. The one thing the early sponsor wanted was product identification. The advertising on every program was concentrated on one product. The listener always associated the product with the theme song and the star. If you are old enough you remember that the song "Smiles" meant the Ipana Troubadours and Ipana Toothpaste; "The Perfect Song," Amos and Andy and Pepsodent Toothpaste; "Two Guitars," Harry Horlick and his A and P Gypsies; "Your Time is My Time," Rudy Vallee and the Fleischman Yeast Hour. . . . Many conferences were held to discuss this important problem. Would advertising two different products on the same program bewilder the average listener? Would people be brushing their teeth with Sal Hepatica and trying to fight off that "logy feeling" by swallowing Ipana?

Our advertising fugleman was a supersalesman. He not only convinced the Bristol-Myers Company that this radical gesture would get results, he also reminded them that combining the two programs would enable the company to save the expense of one orchestra. Tradition may be tradition but business is business. Bristol-Myers intimated that it was a deal if the new show was satisfactory. I remember the day we auditioned the hour show. The Sal Hepatica commercial had the announcer enthusiastically explaining the fizzing that followed the instant the teaspoonful of Sal Hepatica was dropped into the water. A glass of water was held up to the microphone to enable the audience at home to hear the fizzing. After the audition I complimented the soundman. "That Sal Hepatica effect came off fine," I said. Pulling me into a corner he whispered, "Don't say anything, but before the run-through I tried Sal Hepatica in the water and it didn't fizz loud enough over the mike." Whispering back, I said, "But how did you get that perfect effect?"

Looking around to make sure nobody could hear, he chuckled, "I used Bromo Seltzer." Bristol-Myers okayed the audition and signed to sponsor the full hour for their two products: Ipana and Sal Hepatica.

At first the program was called the Hour of Smiles. ("Ipana for the smile of beauty — Sal Hepatica for the smile of health.") This title always sounded to me as though it had been spawned by two badly mated vice-presidents who had gone up-carpet out of season.

Radio as an advertising medium was of great importance in the smaller communities. People in the metropolitan areas were exposed to newspaper, billboard and display advertising and were familiar with the popular highly publicized products. The hinterland was a large and very important market. To get his sales messages over to the people living in small towns the sponsor depended almost entirely on his radio propaganda. It seemed to me that if we had a title that would interest people in small towns, our program would have a wider appeal. *Show Boat* was a very popular show then. Everybody knew what a show boat was and the sort of entertainment it promised. I was sure that almost every small community in America had a town hall. The Hour of Smiles title was returned to the vice-presidents during a lull one day while they were talking about themselves. Our new show, a down-to-earth attraction, was sprinkled with well-water and christened Town Hall Tonight.

The show opened with a small-town band playing. The excitement of the folks could be heard as they arrived to attend their weekly show in the old town hall.

In the script it read something like this:

[30]

Town Hall Opening

ORCHESTRA	"Smile, Darn Yer, Smile . . ."
ANNOUNCER	An Hour of Smiles in Town Hall Tonight, Folks. Sixty minutes of fun and music brought to you by Ipana Toothpaste and Sal Hepatica. Ipana for the Smile of Beauty. Sal Hepatica for the Smile of Health. Fun with our star comedian, Fred Allen. Music by Peter van Steeden. And our special added attraction, the Town Hall Varieties! New Music! New Voices! New Laughs! It's Town Hall Tonight!
ORCHESTRA	"National Emblem March."
ANNOUNCER	Listen to that crowd cheer Fred Allen as he leads the parade to the old Town Hall. Fred's conducting the band with a big sword followed by those dull blades of the boards . . . the Mighty Allen Art Players. Let's join the shouting throng. Everybody's going! Everybody's going!
	(Music up. . . . Fades for . . .)
ANNOUNCER	HERE THEY COME! LOVEBIRDS!
BOY	But I thought we were going to elope, Darling, you haven't packed your things.
GIRL	All I'm taking is you and my radio, Sweetheart. It's Town Hall Tonight!
	(Music up. . . . Fades for . . .)
ANNOUNCER	DETECTIVES!
2ND GIRL	It's terrible. The thieves took my money and jewelry, Officer.

[31]

OFFICER   It could be worse, Lady. Suppose they took your radio. It's Town Hall Tonight!
           (Music up. . . . Fades for . . .)

ANNOUNCER FORTUNE TELLERS!

VOICE   Is my husband out with another woman, Swami?

SWAMI   In my crystal I see your husband home by the radio, Madam. It's Town Hall Tonight!
           (Music up to finish)

ANNOUNCER And here we are before the Old Town Hall . . . and there's Fred exchanging iambic banter with the crowd. Let's listen.

ALLEN   This year's kisses may not taste as sweet, Folks. But we didn't come to neck. We're here to open up the Old Town Hall. Step lively, please.

THE CROWD Hi, Fancy Stockins.

ALLEN   Hello, there, Buster. How's tricks?

VOICE   Evenin, Tunnel-Mouth.

ALLEN   Hi, there, Sister Nag. Taking your dog in to see the show?

VOICE   Yep. And I hope he don't catch no fleas from your actors.

ALLEN   That's what they all say, Folks. You'll laugh. You'll weep. You'll fall asleep. On the inside. So . . . Hurry! Hurry! Hurry!
           (Applause)

After the usual overture the show started inside the Town Hall with a few bulletins or announcements that concerned the various local clubs, the business firms or the strange characters who inhabited the little town.

Pop Mullen, the owner of the lunchwagon on the square, often had special entree or Thanksgiving dinner announcements he wanted the folks to know about. Pop's lunchwagon had one wheel off at the far end and his diners had to eat everything uphill.

The favorite was Hodge White. The radio audience at first thought that Hodge was a name we had made up after taking some liberties with the alphabet. Actually Hodge White was a good friend of mine who ran a small general store in Dorchester, Massachusetts. He was a genial monger of groceries, coal, candy, kerosene, ice cream or anything that would lie still and stay indoors. Hodge had a ready wit that was always ready and he would rather engage a customer in a battle of wits than make a sale.

I lived in Dorchester. When I first went into vaudeville, Hodge began calling me "the ackter." After I had started "Town Hall Tonight" I was kidding Hodge one day. I told him that he should advertise in radio and if he would sponsor me, I would make his name a household word. He said I would have to convince him. I started to read Hodge's announcements every week. Hodge would listen in his store. No customer could make a sound between 9 P.M. and 10 P.M.; when our program was on the air, Hodge refused to sell any sliced meat. When the slicing machine was turned on static started in the radio set. If you wanted any sliced meat you had to wait until our show was over. Hodge used to say "Why should I turn on the meat slicer when I've got a ham on the radio?"

As Hodge's name became known to millions of radio listeners, he found himself enjoying the status of an apprentice celebrity. Tourists coming to Boston would drive out to Dorchester to look at his famous store and to talk to Hodge and get his autograph. I asked Hodge to be a guest on our show many times but he never would make the trip to New York.

Hodge's announcements usually took this form:

ALLEN Thank you, thank you. And good evening, ladies and gentlemen. Now before we look in the oven to see if Uncle Don has left something hot for you kiddies, I'll read you the Town Hall Bulletin for tonight. Hodge White . . . local impresario in charge of classical entertainment . . . announces that the Monte Carlo Ballet will appear here at the Town Hall on Thursday night, and if you're a lover of artistic jumping around you're sure in for a treat. Hodge says that the men can read and the women folks knit during the show and they won't be disturbed by the actors. Hodge saw the ballet up in New York and says it isn't noisy. Most of the time the dancers are loping around on tiptoe. So if you want a nice quiet evening away from home Hodge is recommending the Monte Carlo this Thursday night.

Or:

ALLEN Now, before we back up the wagons so we'll have some place to put the lumber when we bring down the house, I'll read you the Town Hall Bulletin for

tonight. Hodge White . . . manager of the Bijou
Dream Picture Palace . . . says the new picture starting tomorrow will star Gladys Swarthout and Fred
MacMurray. Hodge says in New York City the picture
was called *The Champagne Waltz,* but the Married
Women's Temperance Guild says that if Hodge ad-
vertises the word "champagne" the girls will picket
the theater. So for the two days *The Champagne
Waltz* will be at the Bijou, Hodge is calling it *The
Sarsaparilla Peabody.* So much for censorship around
the square. . . .

Or:

ALLEN Hodge White says kleptomaniacs have been loose
in the store lately and last week when he took inventory four finnan haddie were missing. Hodge
doesn't want to call in the law but he says this fish-
lifting has got to stop. Hodge says you're wasting
your time. He knows who you fish-lifters are, and
you can stuff the finnan haddie in your shirts and
hide them in your bustles, but when you go by the
cash register and the cat looks up, the fish goes on
your bill at the end of the week. So much for deep-
sea duplicity around the square, and now for the
Town Hall news. . . .

Writing a full hour of comedy every week was a chore.
Rudy Vallee, Kate Smith and some others presented hour
shows, but with substantial budgets they could book four or
five acts to help them reduce their sixty minutes to an effort-

less talent cavalcade. We had no money available to enable us to compete with these programs. We had to develop a group of versatile actors and invent features to try to fill the hour with laughs.

One of our features was the Town Hall News. Our Town Hall show was essentially the same type of show that was popular in vaudeville theaters around the country at that time. These shows always started with the news reel. Our version enabled us to comment on topical events and to write burlesque interviews and satirize people currently in the public eye. The Town Hall News soon became quite popular.

The Summer Theater

ALLEN New York City, New York. As the final curtain drops on the Broadway theater this month, many actors turn their attention to the summer playhouse. Little Theater groups spring up in barns and haylofts around the country, affording a haven for actors, producers and directors when activity in the Broadway showshops all but disappears. Town Hall News interviews a group of untalented nobodies identified with obscure bucolic enterprises last season. First a young New York producer who uses the summer theater as a laboratory, Mr. Dawson Bells.

BELLS To me the theater is merely a test tube. In it I brew all human emotions.

ALLEN You are not interested in the audience, Mr. Bells?

BELLS The audience means nothing. The theater means nothing. The play means nothing.

[36]

ALLEN   Only you.

BELLS   Yes. I mean something.

ALLEN   Is that the consensus?

BELLS   I am the consensus. I proved that in my Laboratory Theater during the past season. Did you see my play *Thread?*

ALLEN   No.

BELLS   Two hundred sewing machines on the stage. Sewing, sewing! A silkworm enters. "The machine age," he mutters. The silkworm holds in. The sewing machines stop! Curtain! Think it over.

ALLEN   Yes. I —

BELLS   You saw my play *Crash?*

ALLEN   No. I —

BELLS   The curtain goes up. A bass drum is center stage. The drum is a symbol. On the drum is a cymbal. The cymbal is a symbol. The audience ponders. A termite smacks his lips. Curtain! You see the work I am doing.

ALLEN   You are producing this summer?

BELLS   At Long Crag, Connecticut. I'm doing an Ibsen play in a windmill. The audience rides about in baskets on the four paddles. As the paddles pass the bottom of the windmill, the audience looks in. Snatches of the play are seen.

ALLEN   How do you know what the whole play is about?

BELLS   The windmill stops. The four groups are introduced. They withdraw. Views are exchanged. It dawns on them. The following summer I am presenting a sea-

[37]

son of Shakespeare in a lighthouse off the coast of Old Orchard, Maine. The audience will be in Biddeford, ten miles away.

ALLEN   How will the people know what's going on?

BELLS   The orchestra seats will have telescopes. The balcony seats will have opera glasses.

ALLEN   And the folks in the gallery?

BELLS   They can't see me.

ALLEN   That goes for me, too. And thank you, Mr. Dawson Bells.

The Opening of The World's Fair

ALLEN   Flushing, New York. With flags flying and bands blaring, the New York's World's Fair of 1940 finally opens its gates to an eager and impatient America. Huge signs screaming "Hello, Folks" prove that the Fair has abandoned its high hat and is greeting fairgoers this year in its shirtsleeves. Town Hall News questions visitors on opening day to check on assorted reactions to 1940 World's Fair. The first visitor to misconstrue the spirit of the Fair was Mr. Balzac McGee. You had an embarrassing experience, Mr. McGee?

MCGEE   Yeah. You can go so far at the Fair. And that's all.

ALLEN   How do you mean?

MCGEE   Well, me and the wife seen all that stuff in the papers.

ALLEN   The advance publicity?

MCGEE Yeah. This ain't no high-hat fair. Come in and let your hair down.

ALLEN Be yourself. Relax.

MCGEE Yeah. So I says to the wife, "Gert, let's give this joy spot a whoil."

ALLEN And out you went, eh?

MCGEE Saturday, me and Gert and the kid.

ALLEN What happened?

MCGEE We come in the Fair. Everybody's yellin' "Hello, Folks." Me and Gert and the kid picked it up. The three of us is yelling "Hello, Folks."

ALLEN Getting into the spirit of the Fair, eh?

MCGEE Yeah. A swell-lookin' dame goes over and says "Hello, Folks. Make yerselves to home."

ALLEN And did you?

MCGEE Yeah. I took off me coat. Gert's feet start to hurt; she takes off her shoes. The kid starts bawlin'; we take off his rompers.

ALLEN You must have felt at home.

MCGEE Yeah. Me and Gert's in our stockin' feet. The kid ain't got nothin' on. We're goin' from exhibit to exhibit yellin' "Hello, Folks."

ALLEN What a day, eh?

MCGEE Yeah. Passin' the Borden Exhibit the kid gets hungry.

ALLEN And you —

MCGEE I stepped in and pulled a pint of milk outta one of the cows.

ALLEN Nobody stopped you?

[39]

MCGEE   A guy come runnin' out, but I yelled, "Hello, Folks." He ducks back in.

ALLEN   Fine.

MCGEE   Passin' the Ford Exhibit, Gert is tired.

ALLEN   Did you rest there?

MCGEE   Yeah. Me and Gert and the kid climbed into one of them new sedans and grabbed a little shuteye.

ALLEN   And no one bothered you?

MCGEE   Some guy looks in the sedan. He says, "What's this?" I yells, "Hello, Folks." And he beats it.

ALLEN   This went on all day?

MCGEE   Yeah. We're eatin' samples in the Food Exhibits, Gert calls her old lady from the phone buildin'. The kid is swellin' up from drinkin' free Coca-Cola.

ALLEN   You were really making yourselves at home.

MCGEE   Yeah. We seen we couldn't do the whole Fair in one day. Gert says, "How about stayin' all night?"

ALLEN   A happy thought.

MCGEE   It's okay by me. We pick out a spot to flop and start gettin' ready.

ALLEN   The three of you, eh?

MCGEE   Yeah. I'm sitting by the Lagoon of Nations in me underwear. I'm readin' the paper by the light from the fireworks. When anybody goes by, I'm yellin', "Hello, Folks."

ALLEN   Observing the spirit of the Fair, eh?

MCGEE   And how. Gert's over washin' some stockin's in the Aquacade. The kid's behind the Perisphere doin' somethin'.

[40   ]

ALLEN   Yes.

MCGEE   Then it comes.

ALLEN   What?

MCGEE   I feel a hand on me shoulder. I look up. It's a cop.

ALLEN   A policeman.

MCGEE   Yeah. In one hand he's got Gert. Under his arm he's got the kid. In the other hand he's got me.

ALLEN   What did you do?

MCGEE   I yell "Hello, Folks!" It's no dice. We're bagged. The next thing I know we're in night court.

ALLEN   What did you say to the judge?

MCGEE   I yell, "Hello, Folks!"

ALLEN   What did the judge say to you?

MCGEE   Thirty days.

ALLEN   I see. And after your visit to this year's exposition you would say . . .

MCGEE   You can go so far at the Fair. And that's all.

ALLEN   Thank you, Mr. Balzac McGee.

Unfortunately, there were a few curds in the laughing yogurt. Organizations and people began to identify themselves in our version of the news and our office became a shrine for nondescript members of the legal profession, eager to sue us on behalf of their greasy clients.

A fancied derogatory jibe, involving his metropolis, caused me to apologize to the mayor of Pottsville, Pa. On one show I referred to the rooms in an actors' hotel in Philadelphia as so small "that even the mice were humpbacked." This aroused some zealous local politician who was sleeping in the pork barrel. He stepped out of the barrel and took me to task in print. He claimed that I had spread propaganda to the effect that all Philadelphia hotels had small rooms and that as a result of my roguery the Republican Party was canceling its plans to hold its convention in Philadelphia that year. To appease this fulminating ward heeler, I had to reply to several editorials published in Philadelphia papers. On another occasion a Scotch joke resulted in the arrival of a round robin, signed by 200 Scotsmen, pledging themselves to stop using Sal Hepatica as long as I remained in radio. I was on the air for eighteen years.

People claiming that their names had been used in the news burlesques, and that they had been held up to ridicule, were always threatening to sue. To eliminate this annoyance we invented a set of names to use for comedy characters. Names like Tomtit McGee, Beau Bernstein, Falvey Nishball and hundreds of others. I thought we were safe coining these synthetic cognomens until one summer up in Biddeford, Maine, an old gentleman, a total stranger, stopped me on the street and said, "Mr. Allen, I heard my name on your program last winter. Who sent it in to you?" I said, "What is your name?" The old gentleman answered, "Sinbad Brittle."

But back to the Town Hall News.

Taxes in Hollywood

ALLEN   Hollywood, California. Prominent moving picture comedian protests income tax assessment. Appearing before Federal Board of Tax Appeals, comedian claims that false teeth are tools of his trade,

[42]

and asks $3500 reduction for special false teeth which eliminated the hiss when comedian used the letter *s*. Town Hall News interviews famous Hollywood personalities to get their opinions on present income-tax laws. A Hollywood leading man who is furious at the Tax Appeal Board is Mr. Delsarte Trundle . . .

TRUNDLE   Hollywood has seen the last of Delsarte Trundle. I'm off to Java.

ALLEN   You're going to live in Java, Mr. Trundle?

TRUNDLE   Yes, I have a demitasse plantation there. Au'voir, the Silver Screen!

ALLEN   You had income-tax trouble?

TRUNDLE   Every business expense of mine was thrown out. Riding crops, $200. Thrown out! Mufflers, $700. Thrown out! Toupees, $8000. Thrown out!

ALLEN   You spent $8000 for toupees?

TRUNDLE   Every actor in Hollywood wears toupees. I have 87. They're indispensable to me. There's my tousled toupee for waking up. My matted toupee for the swimming pool. My windblown toupee for yachting. My toupee with the rhinestone part for evening wear.

ALLEN   And none of these was allowed on your income tax?

TRUNDLE   The tax board ruled the toupee was a luxury.

ALLEN   And you —

TRUNDLE   I claim the toupee is overhead! Au 'voir, America! Delsarte Trundle bids you adieu!

ALLEN   And for America . . . au 'voir, Delsarte Trundle.
         And now Town Hall News brings you a scene from
         the Hollywood Board of Tax Appeals. The come-
         dian who protested the ruling on false teeth is
         called to explain. The scene: The Tax Appeal
         Chambers.

REFEREE The Tax Appeal Board is ready. First protest is
         from Mr. Jed Barks. What is this claim of a $3500
         exemption on your income tax?

BARKS   It's for false teeth. I've got five sets of crockery
         at $700 a set. That's $3500.

REFEREE One set of teeth usually suffices for the average
         man, doesn't it?

BARKS   Not in the movies, Mr. Referee. A movie star's gotta
         have different teeth for different moods.

REFEREE You have all of these teeth here with you today?

BARKS   Yeah. One set I'm wearin'. And four sets I got right
         here on the table.

REFEREE Which set is in your mouth?

BARKS   My eatin' teeth.

REFEREE You're not eating now, are you?

BARKS   No. But I'm prepared. If I get nervous I'll start
         bitin' my nails.

REFEREE I see. What is that first set on the table? Exhibit
         One?

BARKS   Those are my loungin' teeth. I just wear 'em around
         the house.

REFEREE Can't you wear that same set making pictures?

BARKS   No. I can't talk in these teeth. They siss. Look, I'll

[44]

show you. I'll put 'em in. Ssssee? I can ssssay nothing without sisssing!

REFEREE   I see. Exhibit Number Two?

BARKS   These are my laughin' teeth. When I laugh in a
picture the sissing teeth fall out. These are bigger.
Look: HA HA HA!

REFEREE   And that third set there?

BARKS   I use these for sneerin'. The laughin' teeth are too
big; I can't curl my lip over 'em. I'll show you how
these sneerin' teeth work. Haha, me proud beauty!
Haha!

REFEREE   Yes, that set is smaller.

BARKS   Right. When I skin my teeth, I can skin plenty for
closeups.

REFEREE   And the last set?

BARKS   These are my gnashin' teeth. They're stronger.
Wait, I'll put 'em in. *(Sound of castanets)* No, I
won't sign them papers! *(Castanet sound again)*
See?

REFEREE   Yes. And you say each set cost you $700?

BARKS   Right. What's the ruling, Mr. Referee?

REFEREE   The Tax Board will allow you the cost of one set of
teeth, Barks. $700 from $3500 — you owe $2800
more on your income tax.

BARKS   But I haven't got the money, Ref!

REFEREE   Then we'll have to hold four sets of your teeth
until the amount is paid.

BARKS   I can't work without all my teeth!

REFEREE   Until the extra tax is paid, the Board is holding your hissing, laughing, sneering and gnashing teeth.

BARKS   Well then, you better hold these, too, Ref.

REFEREE   Your eating teeth!

BARKS   Right. If I can't work, I can't eat. So long!

"Running gags" were very important in radio. A running gag is a comedy bit of business carried over from program to program that will stimulate the listener's interest to the point where he will want to tune in every week to follow the development of the gag. The soap opera daily installments always finish on a note of suspense. The announcer sobs, while trying to control himself — "And as we leave Granny Tucker in the burning cottage her hearing-aid battery conks out. Can Granny hear the crackling of the flames in the next room? Does Granny Tucker know that if she tries to roll out of the cottage through the roaring fire the brake on her wheelchair is locked? Does Granny know what's cooking? Is it Granny? Tune in tomorrow and find out!" The worried listener tunes in the next day to see if Granny has made an ash of herself.

Running gags are difficult to develop on comedy programs. The only reason the audience tunes in a comedy show the next week is to see if the sponsor has fired the comedian who was so unfunny the previous week. We stumbled on a running gag that showed promise. We interviewed a retired fireman who owned a talking mynah bird. The mynah bird looks like a small patent-leather crow. Most of the talking birds repeat words they have been taught. The parrot will say "Polly wants a cracker" only if you start the conversation. The mynah can answer questions. The man we planned to interview would say, "What does Mae West say?" and the bird would answer, "Come up and see me sometime. Come up and see me sometime." The first time the mynah bird appeared it talked all afternoon at rehearsal. It talked all night backstage. But when we were on the air and the bird was brought to the microphone, it was mute. The owner pleaded with the mynah. He threatened it. Nothing audible happened. The audience started laughing. The owner was embarrassed. Finally, I invited him to bring the bird back on the program the next week and we would try again. The following week the bird talked all day and night around the studio. When it was brought to the microphone the owner addressed the mynah with his usual opening line, "What does Mae West say?" The bird not only said nothing — it looked at the owner as though he owed three years' dues to the Audubon Society. Again the bird was speechless. Again there were more threats, more cajoling to no avail. Again I invited the owner back.

For five or six weeks the bird was brought back to the program. It still refused to talk. We were receiving hundreds of letters telling us how to get the bird to talk — "Put out the lights in the studio," "Soak its birdseed in hot milk," and so forth. We were getting newspaper publicity from coast to coast. Some congressman down in Washington had advised another congressman to listen to our bird and learn to shut up.

Just as we had a running gag that had caught the country's fancy, one of the advertising agency executives sent word that the mynah bird would have to be taken off the program. There was a rumor, he intimated, that we had concealed the original bird and were using a feathered decoy to make sure there would be no bird talk. We argued and argued and got no place. We brought in the bird owner, who took an oath that he was bringing back the same mynah bird each week. (Who would have two mynah birds?) Everybody talked except the bird. Trying to move the agency man was like an armless man trying to move his rook in a chess game. He hinted that collusion was on the wing and that he and the advertising agency would not be a party to any flimflam attempt to swindle the great American radio audience.

For the final appearance of the mynah bird we allowed thirty minutes to permit the owner to shout his, "What does Mae West say?" to his heart's content. After about twenty minutes of this solo the mynah bird gave up and answered, "Come up and see me sometime. Come up and see me sometime." Our running gag had run its course. The advertising man was wrong about the feathered decoy, but I learned early in radio never to argue with an executive. I always say, "The only thing you can tell an advertising man is that he is fortunate that he isn't in some other business."

I still had faith in the running gag and later, when I was trying to conjure up a job for a friend of mine, I found another version. This was Professor Quigley, the world's greatest escape artist.

We introduced Professor Quigley to the radio audience in this manner:

Professor Quigley

ALLEN   And now, ladies and gentlemen, we bring you the greatest novelty ever to appear in radio . . . Professor

Quigley. Professor Quigley is an escape artist, and tonight he will permit himself to be nailed in a packing case, which we have here at the microphone. You will see and hear him nailed up, and in full view of the audience Professor Quigley will escape. Have you been an escape artist for long, Professor?

QUIGLEY For thirty years, Mr. Allen.

ALLEN Where have you done most of your escaping?

QUIGLEY In vaudeville, smoke-talks, psychopathic wards.

ALLEN Psychopathic wards?

QUIGLEY I was there professionally. Escaping from strait-jackets and other contraptions.

ALLEN I see. And tonight, Professor Quigley, you are making your first escape over the radio?

QUIGLEY Yes, I'm going to escape from this packing case in three minutes flat.

ALLEN Our time is limited, Professor. I want it understood that if you don't escape in three minutes we'll have to go on with the show.

QUIGLEY Professor Quigley never fails. If I do not escape in three minutes I am giving fifty dollars to charity.

ALLEN Fine. Now you can go right ahead, if you will.

QUIGLEY I demand a full three minutes.

ALLEN Yes, yes, Professor. *(Professor gets into box)* Uncle Jim is going to nail you up and Harry Von Zell will hold the watch. You'll get the full three minutes, no more, no less. *(Sound of hammer and nails)* Professor Quigley is being nailed in, folks. You've got the watch, Harry?

[49]

HARRY   Yes, ten seconds already, Fred.

ALLEN   Let's go, Professor. Ladies and gentlemen, the Professor is nailed in a solid packing case. There is a heavy clasp and padlock on one side of the box, and the top has been nailed down securely. How is the time, Harry?

HARRY   Forty-five seconds exactly, Fred.

ALLEN   I'm going to move the microphone down, ladies and gentlemen, and try to get Professor Quigley to say a few words to you from inside the box. *(Tapping box)* Professor Quigley?

QUIGLEY   *(Inside box)* Yes . . . I'm busy.

ALLEN   I know you're busy, Professor, but will you say a few words to the radio audience?

QUIGLEY   Okay. Hello folks, it's dark in here.

HARRY   One minute, Fred.

ALLEN   One minute, Professor.

QUIGLEY   Okay. Everything's coming along fine. I'll be right home, Ma!

ALLEN   Thank you, Professor. Ladies and gentlemen, you have been listening to Professor Quigley, speaking to you from inside the packing case. The Professor has only two more minutes to go but he's in there working quietly.

HARRY   Do you think he'll make it, Fred?

ALLEN   If the Professor isn't worried, I'm not. Any sign of him coming out on your side, Harry?

HARRY   No, Fred. Something just flew out of a knothole. It looked like a moth.

[50]

ALLEN   The Professor probably took his coat off and woke the moth up. How much time?

HARRY   Two minutes gone.

ALLEN   One minute to go, ladies and gentlemen. I'll just make sure the Professor is all right. One more minute, Professor!

QUIGLEY Okay.

ALLEN   How are you doing?

QUIGLEY Time out, time out! I dropped my glasses!

ALLEN   We can't take time out, Professor. You've got just three minutes.

QUIGLEY I can't see what I'm doing!

ALLEN   Can't you escape from memory?

HARRY   *(Off mike)* Two minutes and thirty seconds.

QUIGLEY *(Yells)* TIME OUT, TIME OUT!

ALLEN   We can't stop, Professor. If you're not out in three minutes we'll have to open the box, that's all.

QUIGLEY Don't open this box. I'll get a lawyer!

ALLEN   Get a lawyer. You're supposed to be out in three minutes flat. Get ready with the chisel, Harry.

HARRY   Ready, Fred. It's just three minutes now.

ALLEN   Open the box!

QUIGLEY Get away from here! *(Sound of box being pried open)*

HARRY   The Professor's going to be pretty mad, Fred.

ALLEN   He'll have to be mad, Harry. You heard him say he'd be out in three minutes. The three minutes are up and where is he?

[51]

QUIGLEY *(Out of box)* Here I am. This is an outrage. My repu-
tation is ruined!

ALLEN Now just a minute, Professor . . .

QUIGLEY I dropped my glasses! I demanded time out! You
can't do this to me!

ALLEN Listen, we have other acts on this show, Professor.
I told you that before you got into the box.

QUIGLEY I had one leg out. I would have escaped. I dropped
my glasses.

ALLEN I'm sorry, Professor, we can't give you any more time
tonight.

QUIGLEY I didn't get the full three minutes!

ALLEN Well, there's only one thing we can do. If you want
to come back next Wednesday and try it again,
we'll arrange to give you more time. How is that?

QUIGLEY Next Wednesday? Right here?

ALLEN Yes, Professor. I'm sorry things got mixed up tonight. But we'll be glad to have you escape next
Wednesday.

QUIGLEY I'll be here!

Professor Quigley had trouble every week. On his second
attempt to break the escape record, after he had been nailed
in the box, a policeman suddenly appeared in the studio.
Somebody had parked a car near a hydrant outside the NBC
studios. The policeman questioned me and the others on the
program. None of us knew anything about the parked car.
I thought about the professor. He shouted from the confines
of the box that the car was his. He asked for just a minute

until he finished escaping. The policeman was adamant. He started to take out a ticket. We pried the top off the box to permit the professor to get his car away from the hydrant in time. The next week, after the professor had been nailed in, a truck driver arrived. He had delivered the box and claimed that the box had never been paid for. The lumber company was taking the box back. It was too late at night to find some NBC executive who could take action. The box, with the professor inside, was carried away. The following week the truck driver was back with the box. There had been a great mistake. The truck driver apologized and left. When we opened the box a complete stranger stepped out. He was a Hindu magician who had been escaping the previous week at a small theater uptown and had had his wooden escape box repossessed, also. We nailed the Hindu back in the box, called the truck driver and demanded that Professor Quigley be returned the following week.

At this crucial juncture my friendly helper, the executive in the advertising agency who had liquidated the mynah bird, had another suggestion. This one liquidated the escape artist. I often wonder what happened to Professor Quigley. The gag had just started to attract attention when it had to be abandoned because the executive thought it was getting tiresome.

The reaction to the mynah bird and Professor Quigley gags convinced me that if we could ever get the ideal device radio would welcome it with open ears.

Our most popular running gag, the one that created the most excitement, was the feud between Jack Benny and myself. The feud with Jack started accidentally. A little boy named Stewart Canin, whose hobby was being a violin virtuoso, appeared on our program. After he had stopped the show playing a very difficult number, "The Flight of the Bumble Bee," I complimented him. I told the boy about Mr. Benny, an ancient and rancid violinist who lived out in Hollywood, and I said that if Mr. Benny had heard this tyke's rendition of "The Bee" he should hang his head in symphonic shame and pluck the horsehairs out of his bow and return them to the tail of the stallion from which they had been taken.

The next week, on his program, Mr. Benny insulted me openly, and mildly applauded the little boy's rendition. Mr. Benny informed me that "The Bee" was in his repertoire and he would be happy to render "The Bee" the instant any music lover requested it. On my next program, posing as a music lover, I requested it. Then the battle was on. Jack and I didn't plan anything. I didn't want to explain that I thought it would be good for us. The Jack Benny program was the highest-rated show in radio at that time. With our smaller audience it would take an academy award display of intestinal fortitude to ask Jack to participate in a feud with me. I would be hitching my gaggin' to a star. All I could do was to hope that Jack would have some fun with the idea and that it could be developed.

While I was hoping, we picked on Jack on Town Hall Tonight in this fashion:

Jack Benny Feud

PICKET *(Fading in)* This program is unfair to Jack Benny. This program is unfair to Jack Benny . . .

PORTLAND   Is that a picket, Mr. Allen?

ALLEN   If it isn't, it's a man talking to himself for my benefit.

PICKET   Don't listen to this program. It's unfair to Jack Benny.

PORTLAND   Gosh. Do you think Jack belongs to a union?

ALLEN   If he does it isn't the musicians' union. While I think of it, did you hear Mr. B. last Sunday?

PORTLAND   Yes, Jack had a great program, didn't he?

ALLEN   You don't think it was any better just because it was coming out of the Waldorf, do you? I'll bet he won't get his program in there next Sunday without baggage.

PORTLAND   Jack didn't pull any *faux pas* at the Waldorf, did he?

ALLEN   Coming out he saw a lot of empty finger-bowls stacked up on a table. He'd never seen a finger-bowl before. He said, "Gosh, the next war is going to be terrible. They're making trench hats for children!"

PORTLAND   Maybe Jack's mad at you because you said he was anemic.

ALLEN   He is anemic. When a mosquito lands on Benny all he gets is practice.

PORTLAND   He is pretty white all right.

ALLEN   White! If you put a piece of celery alongside that guy the celery looks like rhubarb.

PICKET   This program is unfair to Jack Benny. This program . . .

ALLEN   Hey. Just a minute, friend . . .

PICKET   Don't call me friend, Buddy. I may be only a picket but I'm particular.

PORTLAND   Did someone send you over to picket Mr. Allen?

PICKET   Yeah. I got my orders from a certain party.

ALLEN   What's his name?

PICKET   It's a trade secret, Buddy.

ALLEN   Was it an emaciated movie star whose hobby is losing his violin at crucial moments?

PICKET   I can't mention no names, but yer warm.

PORTLAND   It's Jack all right, Mr. Allen.

PICKET   If Jack's his first name he ought to change it to Chickenfeed.

ALLEN   How much is he paying you to picket me?

PICKET   Fifty cents an hour. And I'm breakin' in these shoes for him while I'm walkin'.

PORTLAND   Gosh. Only fifty cents an hour!

PICKET   Yeah. He said the job was picketin' a microphone. I could take short steps.

ALLEN   That's Benny. He's not only anemic, he's cheap. If he ever gets his hands on all the nickels in this country the buffalo will become extinct.

PICKET   He's pretty tight all right, Bud. For a down payment he showed me a dollar bill. Washington was so ashamed bein' in that company he was hanging his head on the buck. But he's gonna gimme five bucks.

[56]

PORTLAND   When?

PICKET   He said he'd pay me the night he plays "The Bee."

ALLEN   Well, the money might come in handy in your old age.

PORTLAND   You ought to hire a picket and get even, Mr. Allen.

ALLEN   I will. Here's ten dollars, son.

PICKET   Thanks, Mr. Allen. You ain't no violin player, you're a gentleman.

ALLEN   There is a distinction, yes.

PICKET   What do you want me to do for this dough, croak that B Flat Kubelik?

ALLEN   No, just picket him. Here's ten dollars more. Picket him thoroughly.

PICKET   Listen, that guy'll see so many pickets he'll think he's livin' behind a fence. . . . So long!

ALLEN   So long.

Radio in the 30's was a calm and tranquil medium. Oleaginous-voiced announcers smoothly purred their commercial copy into the microphones enunciating each lubricated syllable. Tony Wons was cooing his soothing poems. Bedtime stories were popular. Radio was one unruffled day from Cheerio in the early morning through to Music to Read By at midnight. Radio was fraught with politeness. No voice was ever raised in public.

When Jack and I started to ignore precedent and bellow

[57]

censored Billingsgate at each other, the radio audience perked up. It was akin to dropping a mongoose into a snake pit — things started coming to life.

The feud gained momentum. After two years of vituperative exchanges the mail was bigger than ever. Many people took the arguing seriously. Jack's supporters were writing to insult me. My followers were busy sending poison pen fanmail to Jack. When the wrangling had reached its peak it posed problems. When I went home to Dorchester to see my aunt I had to wait until it was dark before it was safe to venture into her neighborhood. On one trip I went out to see my aunt during the afternoon. One of the neighbors must have seen me. In no time the entire neighborhood knew I was visiting my aunt. (Long before radar my aunt's neighbors were beaming gossip to each other with uncanny speed.) When school got out about forty kids gathered in front of my aunt's house and demanded that I look out. Rather than have them tip over the house with my aunt in it, I opened the window and yelled, "What do you kids want?" Forty shrill voices shrieked, "You gotta beat Jack Benny for Dorchester, Fred. Kill Jack Benny! Beat his brains out!" At Waukegan, I imagine kids with shrill voices were suggesting that Jack ditto me.

Finally, when our synthetic invective had reached a crescendo, Jack challenged me to a fight. I accepted the challenge. We both started training on our programs. Joe Louis, the heavyweight champion, appeared on my show to help me plan my strategy. Jack was taking transfusions and training in a phone booth with two wildcats.

One of our Town Hall Tonight scripts at this time explains my attitude:

Training for the Allen-Benny Fight

PORTLAND   Are you going to train to fight Jack Benny?

ALLEN   Yes, Portland, I'll have to go on a pastry diet. I'll do some soft living to get in the same condition; I don't want to take an unfair advantage. Benny's as soft as a herd of goo.

HARRY   Jack said you had to starch your legs so they wouldn't wobble, Fred.

ALLEN   I don't have to wear a ramrod in the back of my vest to keep my spine from drooping. If Benny ever gets into the ring with me he'd better bring a taxidermist for his second. If I hit him once he'll be the life of the observation ward.

HARRY   What about Benny's muscles?

ALLEN   His arm looks like a buggy whip with fingers. I've got veins in my nose bigger than Benny's arm. And as for those legs. I've seen better-looking legs on a bridge table. Benny with those vegetarian gams!

HARRY   Has Jack got vegetarian legs, Fred?

ALLEN   Has he? Where there should be a calf, Benny's got aspic. At a cannibal dinner Benny wouldn't even be on the menu. I'll knock that guy so cold he'll think he's something Admiral Byrd left behind.

PORTLAND   Jack said on his program he saved your life in vaudeville.

ALLEN   Nobody saved my life in vaudeville. I died everywhere. The first time I met Benny was in Elyria, Ohio. He was doing a monologue with a pig on the stage.

PORTLAND   A pig?

ALLEN   Yes. The pig was there to eat up the stuff the audience threw at Benny. It was in his contract that he had to leave the stage the way he found it. Some weeks he used to use two pigs.

PORTLAND   What kind of an act was Jack doing then, Mr. Allen?

ALLEN   It was one of those acts. It wasn't safe to take a deep breath while he was on. He used to open the act throwing his violin on the stage. Then, if nothing happened, Benny came on.

HARRY   And Jack didn't save your life?

ALLEN   I saved his life. I'll never forget it. Benny was out on the stage in his spangled tights playing the violin. His big number was Pony Boy. He just started to play Pony Boy when a man in the front row started to shoot.

HARRY   A Westerner?

ALLEN   No, a music lover. I ran out on the stage in front of Jack. I thought the star running on might save his life. In the excitement Benny stole two bows and I was shot in the chest. They took me to the hospital.

PORTLAND   Is that when Jack gave you the transfusion?

ALLEN   Yes, Portland. They told me in the hospital later. It was the first time at a transfusion the donor ever asked for a receipt for his blood.

HARRY   Did the transfusion help you?

ALLEN   I had a relapse. Then as a result of the Benny transfusion I had anemia for two years. And it affected me in other ways. I couldn't get my hand in my money pocket for months. I found myself window shopping at toupee stores. It was terrible.

HARRY   How do you fight, Fred? Do you come out punching?

ALLEN   Benny'll think he's a time clock, Harry.

HARRY   I hear Benny can take a lot of body punishment.

ALLEN   He's a pan dowdy with skin on. Benny's stomach hangs down like a Jello knapsack. I'll frappe him. Mr. Benny, I am at your service.

After weeks of wrangling about the site, Jack and I finally agreed to do physical battle and dismantle each other anatomically on his program. A date was selected and duly publicized on both programs. The demand for broadcast tickets was so great that NBC had no studio in Radio City large enough to accommodate the listeners who were eager to witness the bloodletting. They probably thought they were going to see a real fight. The combatants were two rare specimens. Jack's legs looked like two swan's necks with the feathers plucked. I was in such bad shape I would get winded if I ran a fever. The day of the joust arrived. On Sunday, March 14, 1937, the broadcast was held in the ballroom at the Pierre Hotel. The audience was in a mood of anticipation. Jack and I were given ovations. During the first part of the program people were laughing at straight lines, they couldn't wait for the jokes. After Jack had finished his routines with Don, Mary and Schlepperman and had committed a singing commercial personally, I made my entrance. The dialogue frankly didn't live up to the pandemonium. After a heated exchange with Jack the script read:

JACK	That means fight where I come from.
FRED	You mean your blood would boil if you had any.
JACK	Yes, and I've got just enough to resent that. Mr. Allen, I come from the West. I'm a hard-ridin', two-fisted he-man, and if you'll step out in the hallway I'm ready to settle this little affair man to man.
FRED	You are, eh?
JACK	Yeah. Do you want to go through with this?
FRED	Don't stall, Benny. Where's the hallway — where's the door?
JACK	Now, listen here, Allen. I'll give you just one more chance to apologize.
FRED	Apologize? Why I'll knock you flatter than the first eight minutes of this program.
JACK	You asked for it, Allen. Let's go!

(We hear them stamping out of the room)

JACK   Hm, I'm sorry now I sold my rowing machine.
                 (Door slams)

ORCHESTRA   "Love and Learn"

Following the musical number, Mary and Don described how
Jack and I were at each other's throats out in the hallway.
Our footsteps were heard — and the script reads:

                 (Door opens)

JACK   Ha . . ha . . ha! Gosh, Freddie, those were the
               days, weren't they?

FRED   You're a card, Jackie. Remember that time in
               Toledo when you walked into the magician's
               dressing room and stole his pigeons?

JACK   Do I? They tasted pretty good, didn't they,
               Freddie?

Everything ended on a happy note and the reaction to the
program was excellent. Everybody seemed to be satisfied.
Radio survey figures showed that only one other broadcast,
up to that time, had attracted more listeners — one of President Roosevelt's Fireside Chats. Jack and I heckled each other
for many seasons and eventually made a picture together
called *Love Thy Neighbor*. The feud did do two things —
it improved Jack's violin playing: he told me later that he
had to practise for months to be able to play "The Bee" on
his program; and the association with Jack increased our
listening audience greatly.

When I started the hour show there was so much more time

available it seemed only fair that Portland be allotted some additional minutes. We couldn't lengthen the brief comedy exchanges we had done on the earlier programs. With a short budget we were also short of actors, and gradually our announcer, Harry von Zell, and our orchestra leader, Peter Van Steeden, began playing comedy characters to augment the cast.

To garnish Portland's participation in the festivities we had her arrive with troublesome brats, obnoxious salesmen, insane inventors or any sort of pest we could think of who might upset me. We used this feature for several years and a number of the characters, who later became famous, were introduced by Portland in her madhouse routines.

A typical Portland visit to the Town Hall would affect me like this:

Portland and Her Friends

PORTLAND You remember Mr. Katz and Mr. Binns, Mr. Allen.

ALLEN Yes. I've prayed for amnesia but it didn't help.

KATZ I am managing director, mine host, at the continental joy spot in the Catskilss: Chez Katz.

BINNS I'm operatin' the only Monte Carlo a stone's throw from Trenton: The Sea Gull Manor.

PORTLAND If you still haven't decided where to go, Mr. Allen . . .

KATZ Come to Chez Katz where Park Avenue is meeting the East Side.

BINNS You mean where Riff is meeting Raff, don't you?

KATZ Listen, knocker. Chez Katz is catering to the upper set. You are not getting in without underwear.

BINNS   If all your guests looked out of the window at once you couldn't tell that joint from an egg crate.

ALLEN   On a hot day a resort like that is apt to hatch.

BINNS   At the Sea Gull Manor, brother, comfort is king.

KATZ   Fooey! In a two-dollar room, if you are getting up in the middle of the night you are getting up in the middle of the ocean.

PORTLAND   You mean the tide comes right into the rooms, Mr. Katz?

KATZ   You have got to treading water to get undressed. Confidentially, the chambermaids have webbed feet.

BINNS   That's a lie, Katz!

ALLEN   How does your house detective get around, Binns? With an outboard motor?

BINNS   A high-class resort don't need no house detective. Our guests is under the honor system.

PORTLAND   Well, the mountains and the sea are both good, Mr. Allen.

ALLEN   What about recreation?

KATZ   At Chez Katz you could ping with ponging the whole day through. At night I am running a small pinochle game for high flyers.

BINNS   You can check out of my place ready for the Olympic Games. We got the only sunken golf course in the world. Nine holes when the tide is out.

KATZ   You couldn't get drowned in the mountains.

BINNS   And you won't get starved to death at the sea.

ALLEN   Are you skimping with the vitamins, Katz?

KATZ   Skimping! If you ain't got high blood pressure by
               me in two meals, you are dining au gratin.

BINNS   Listen, Allen. The Sea Gull Manor wins the table
               d'hôte Pulitzer Prize every summer. We gotta beat
               epicures away from the dining room with a black-
               jack.

PORTLAND   Gosh. That sounds tempting, Mr. Allen.

ALLEN   Yes. If I could rent a stomach for a few days I'd
               like to give the cuisine an audition.

KATZ   Before you are making a decision, buddy . . . if
               you can spare an afternoon I would enjoy reading
               you mine special Tidbit Luncheon menu.

BINNS   What have you got? Twenty names for hash?

KATZ   Hash, he's saying! By your chef, hash is a dessert.

PORTLAND   What's on your Tidbit Luncheon menu, Mr. Katz?

KATZ   First, we are serving three napkins, the soup
               shouldn't go through to your vest.

ALLEN   Never mind the precautions. What about the
               food?

KATZ   You are sitting down to the table. Before you can
               say Granville Thomaschefsky the waiter is slap-
               ping a poached egg with herring at you. Before
               you are throwing the last bone on the floor . . .
               BANG! You are looking on a mound of chicken
               liver, Spanish style. You are turning your head,
               and presto!

PORTLAND   Presto change-o?

KATZ   No. Presto chicken! With noodles akimbo, South-

[66]

	ern style. You are getting so many vegetables we are putting a scarecrow in the middle of the table.
BINNS	What you need is a ptomaine specialist.
KATZ	Quiet. No sooner is the wishbone of the chicken visible to the naked eye, then you are confronted with a heaping plate of shmetana concealing blintzes à la Montmarte. This you are topping off with Bronx Tamales à la mode . . . with piping hot tea and lemon.
ALLEN	That's the Tidbit Luncheon?
KATZ	Yes. This we are serving at the snack bar.
BINNS	I give up. After that one of my meals would sound like an hors d'œuvre.
KATZ	For dinner, we are putting it on a little.
ALLEN	No more for me, thanks.
PORTLAND	Yes, my ears have got indigestion, just listening.
KATZ	If we are not killing you with kindness, Allen, a meal like this should do the trick. I will be hearing from you, buddy.
ALLEN	If I ever eat that luncheon, you're bound to.

Advertising agency executives who supervise the presentation of radio shows for their clients have to check on the writers, the weekly scripts, attend rehearsals, worry about the rating and on occasion try to cope with temperamental stars. The executive in charge of our show was a neurotic specimen. He was so high-strung he could have gone to a masquerade as a tennis racquet. He had a long neck that looked as though it were concealing three Adam's apples. Actually he only had one Adam's apple; the other two lumps in his neck were olives he had been too busy to swallow as he dashed down his double Martinis at lunch. This man used to talk to himself incessantly. We called him the one-man conference.

This gentleman nursed two secret ambitions. The first was to put a day bed in his office so that he wouldn't have to sleep sitting up during conferences. His second and greater ambition was to keep changing elements we had in the program. He was always eager to try a new singer, get another quartet, audition a different-type announcer or upset anything the minute we had gotten it running smoothly.

One summer, just before we left the air to start our vacations, the one-man conference called a meeting. The show, he announced, needed something new for the fall. We could mull it over while we were away. Fortunately, I had been thinking about an idea for months. Radio was reaching millions of people living in small towns who never had an opportunity to visit a big city like New York. I thought it might be interesting for small-town folks to meet little people working at unusual jobs in New York City.

This feature was called People You Didn't Expect to Meet. The city was combed for men and women practising strange professions or engaged in odd occupations. Some of the unique artisans we brought to the program were A Lady Blacksmith, A Goldfish Doctor, A Sausage Stuffer, A Worm Salesman, A Canary Specialist, The Last Hurdy-Gurdy Player in Manhattan, A Smoke Watcher, A Tea Taster, etc. These people were not radio-broken. As the season progressed they presented a number of problems. When Mayor LaGuardia

coined an edict banning the hurdy-gurdy from the streets of
New York City we enticed a hurdy-gurdy soloist to appear on
our program in rebuttal. After the script had been written
we discovered that the hurdy-gurdy virtuoso could not read.
The program's troubleshooter "Uncle Jim" Harkins was as-
signed to the case. For several days Mr. Harkins visited the
hurdy-gurdy man's home in Brooklyn and helped him memo-
rize the entire interview. At the dress rehearsal, on the day of
the show, we realized that the interview was too long. We
couldn't cut or change a line. The hurdy-gurdy maestro had
memorized it word for word. That was the way it was done
on the air. Another People You Didn't Expect to Meet guest
the audience never got to. This character was The Champion
Bootblack of the world. On the day of the show, he was kid-
napped. A mysterious voice kept calling us at the studio.
The voice said that it was the Mafia and unless the bootblack's
salary was doubled he would not appear. It wasn't and he
didn't. One guest thought that the rehearsal was the show.
After the rehearsal, he went home and I haven't seen him
since.

People You Didn't Expect to Meet became very popular.
The people interviewed were not ridiculed. I merely discussed
their daily routines, their problems and the performance of
their unconventional chores. As far as I know this was the
first interview series to bring men and women with unusual
professions to the microphone. This is indeed a sorry distinction to claim. Today, radio and television are both cluttered
with tattered extroverts clawing each other to get to the
microphones and cameras to flaunt their grief or to outdull

each other with morbid stories that glorify their piddling functions.

The two boys writing the program with me at this time were Arnold Auerbach and Herman Wouk. Arnold and Herman were classmates at Columbia. After graduation they decided to take up radio writing. Their first working year they spent with Dave Freedman. Dave was a very competent writer. When radio came along he lowered his standards and started thinking in terms of pelf. Dave wrote the first Eddie Cantor scripts but as radio mushroomed he started turning out five or six weekly shows for other comedians. He had voluminous files in which thousands of jokes were catalogued. Dave hired apprentice writers whose jobs were to comb the files for jokes. If a program locale was a lawyer's office, the novice writers would find and assemble fifty or sixty legal, lawyer, accident and judge jokes. These would be turned over to Dave and he would routine them. The fifty or sixty jokes strung together constituted a program.

After their neophyte period had passed Arnold and Herman felt that they were living dogs' lives. Actually, they were retrievers bringing back jokes to the master. They agreed that they were not making any progress. The boys wanted to write and have an opportunity to invent plots and create and develop comedy situations. They submitted a sketch to us and as soon as the sketch was read they went to work. They were conscientious craftsmen and took great pride in their work. Our association was very pleasant and the boys remained with us until the war started. Arnold went into the army, Herman into the navy. In recent years both have prospered. Arnold has written a number of hit Broadway revues — *Call Me Mister, Inside U.S.A.* and *Bless You All.* Herman has written a number of successful books and recently a sensational best seller, *The Caine Mutiny.*

One of the unusual chores Arnold and Herman had to perform on our program was to arrange the first meeting and conduct the initial interviews with the unusual characters. If you want to read something that the author of *The Caine Mutiny* was busy writing during the week of March 15, 1939, I can recommend highly the following interview with a Person You Didn't Expect to Meet:

ALLEN   And now, ladies and gentlemen, I know you didn't expect to meet . . . Dr. Harry F. Nimphius. For many years he has been the official veterinary surgeon at both the Central Park and Prospect Park Zoos. His cage-side manner is highly spoken of by convalescent gorillas and ailing hippopotami alike. Good evening, Dr. Nimphius.

DOCTOR   Good evening, Fred.

ALLEN   I think before we start one thing should be thoroughly understood, Doctor. You're not going to charge us for this visit tonight?

DOCTOR   No, Fred, this is purely a social call.

ALLEN   Fine. Now, Doctor, you're the veterinary surgeon at both the Central Park and Prospect Park Zoos: how long have you held this duplex medical post?

DOCTOR   Twenty-three years.

ALLEN   Twenty-three years. I guess when you started Bear

Mountain was only a cub. Tell me, Doctor, who are some of the carnivorous invalids you have restored to health?

DOCTOR I've treated lions, tigers, leopards, hippos, elephants, zebras.

ALLEN In other words, you've administered first aid to about anything that walks on more than two feet. What, in your estimation, is the chief cause of sickness among your caged clientele?

DOCTOR The public, Fred.

ALLEN You mean the animals keep looking at the people until they can't stand it and neurotic disintegration sets in?

DOCTOR No, but many people think it's funny to feed all kinds of trash to animals. Cigar butts, razor blades, fruitskins, pieces of wire, bottle caps — almost anything you can think of.

ALLEN I thought gastronomic donations were prohibited at all zoos. There are signs about.

DOCTOR I know. But the feeding is always done when the keeper's back is turned. If those people only knew the harm they did to the animals they'd never feed them at all.

ALLEN That's true. Tell me, Doctor, what surgical operations are most common among the animals? Have you ever taken out a giraffe's tonsils or a mink's adenoids?

DOCTOR No. But I *have* treated a lion for ingrown toenails. You see, Fred, when a lion is confined his nails grow

[72]

to extreme lengths and cause him to limp around in pain. I amputate the claw that's causing the trouble.

ALLEN   Does Leo resent having the privacy of his toes invaded? You do take some precautions?

DOCTOR   Oh yes. First, the lion is roped. Then he's given a large piece of wood to bite on.

ALLEN   The wood is a stand-in for you?

DOCTOR   No. It distracts the lion and keeps him from biting the rope in two. Meantime, as a further precaution, he's securely bound with other ropes.

ALLEN   You don't actually start your chiropody until the patient is practically a bundle. How does the lion feel about this hempen approach? Does he sense you are trying to ease his pain?

DOCTOR   Yes, after one of these operations I've had the lion try to lick my hand.

ALLEN   I wouldn't trust a lion, Doctor. He might lick your hand off up to the elbow. Tell me, Doctor, does either zoo own a beast that has been noted for its beauty?

DOCTOR   Yes, we had a buffalo named Dick. He was so perfect his head was used as the model for the buffalo nickel. Dick died about three months ago.

ALLEN   He probably died of a broken heart when those Jefferson nickels came out. Doctor, what amount of food is consumed in one day, say, at the Central Park Zoo?

DOCTOR   400 pounds of meat, 8 bushels of fresh vegetables,

1 bushel of assorted fruit, 10 bales of hay, 5 bags of oats, 30 quarts of milk, and 50 pounds of fresh fish.

ALLEN   And an occasional keeper or two, for dessert?

DOCTOR   No, our animals get plenty to eat, Fred.

ALLEN   I know. But most wild animals have a tendency to consider the human race a snack bar. I heard about a keeper at some zoo who stepped in to feed a leopard and was never heard of again. Two weeks later the leopard hiccuped some brass buttons, but the keeper, in part or in toto, remained apparently an abdominal recluse. But since we're on the subject of food, Doctor, which animal's diet receives the most attention?

DOCTOR   The monkey's, Fred. Unlike the other animals, the monkey is fed four times a day.

ALLEN   That smacks of gluttony, Doctor. What does the simian diet consist of?

DOCTOR   Well, for breakfast a monkey has bread and milk, or cereal. At ten o'clock he gets a large dish of fruit.

ALLEN   He has lunch, of course. It's on the City?

DOCTOR   Yes. The luncheon menu is boiled rice, sweet potatoes, lettuce, and spinach. At three o'clock he gets celery and more fruit.

ALLEN   Passé bananas, etc.?

DOCTOR   No, our monkeys get the best fruits: cherries, strawberries, melons, or perhaps peaches.

ALLEN   And Lew Lehr says monkeys are crazy. Doctor, I am going to ask you a great favor.

DOCTOR   Yes, Fred?

[74]

ALLEN   If things get tough for me around here, I'm tying a tail on myself, going up to the zoo, and telling the chimpanzee to move over.

DOCTOR   And what is the favor, Fred?

ALLEN   If you're going by someday and see me in one of the cages: no cracks!

DOCTOR   I won't, Fred . . . and good night.

ALLEN   And thank you, and good night, Dr. Harry S. Nimphius.

The Mighty Allen Art Players were born of necessity. When this motley band of thespians was named we were still operating with a sharecropper's budget. Guests and big name stars were out of the question. To facilitate the writing we had to break the show down into four parts — The News Reels, People You Didn't Expect to Meet, Portland's specialty and the final comedy sketch. Each week, we had to write sixty minutes of material: interviews, sketches, comedy dialogue, along with the musical and commercial announcements. Continuing these same features from week to week enabled us to salvage comedy lines and situations. Anything left over one week was fodder for the next. If the News Reel spot was too long any item deleted became part of the news the following program. If good lines had to be taken out of a Portland routine they were saved to be used on a future show.

Our actors were extremely versatile. Each of them was an accomplished dialectician. We could write sketches of any type; cast and perform them creditably. Many years ago, every community in the country had a stock company playing repertoire in its local theater. The old Town Hall really had a stock company. All the company lacked was a name. In a moment of creative abandon, I named them the Mighty Allen Art Players.

As the Town Hall Tonight programs came tumbling off the assembly line we tried to vary our product. For several years we presented amateurs. Our microphone welcomed talent in embryo that later grew to be Frank Sinatra, Joan Edwards, Connie Haines, Bob Eberle and a number of others. Later, we replaced the amateurs with Talent of Tomorrow. During this series we saw Beatrice Kaye, Jerry Colonna and Garry Moore pass by going places.

The Mighty Allen Art Players, continuing our tradition, were constantly varying their product. They found themselves performing British society comedies, Russian folk plays, hill-billy court trials, mysteries — some solved by the famous Chinese detective One Long Pan — burlesques on Big Business, and satires on the fads, foibles and favorites of the day.

One of the national favorites was Major Bowes. When the Major's Amateur Hour first appeared in radio he became its biggest attraction. His wheel of fortune and his slogan "Round and round it goes and where it stops nobody knows" were known to every man, woman and child in America. Thousands of amateurs came to New York City from all corners of the country to sample fame under the Major's wing. The winning amateurs on the programs were sent out in units to make personal appearances. At one time the Major Bowes units were singing and dancing in every metropolis and hamlet in the land.

Major Bowes was a shrewd businessman. His publicity man covered the country ballyhooing the Major, his program, his philanthropy and his units. Chambers of Commerce, mayors of large cities and important dignitaries of smaller towns were interviewed to stimulate interest in the Major's projects. Each week, the program saluted what the Major called "the Honor City." If Centralia, Illinois, was "the Honor City," the mayor of Centralia sent in a letter complimenting the Major's good work, and telling what a great community Centralia was. As the Major read these tributes to himself his voice would blush and he would publicly thank the mayor and the people of Centralia. The Major would then give a short history of the city, its location and its principal industries, and accept a badge as an honorary policeman or eighty feet of hose from the Centralia fire chief. Interest was fomented locally in each "Honor City" and the Major handled these presentations very well.

One week, the Mighty Allen Art Players saluted the Major in this fashion:

ALLEN   And now, ladies and gentlemen, to prove that you don't have to break a mirror to start your bad luck, we present the Mighty Allen Art Players. Tonight they present a true-to-life drama of the radio studios. It's called *The Honor City, or It Can Happen Here.* Overture, Peter.

ORCHESTRA   *(Overture . . . Fades out)*

ANNOUNCER   And now Station HIJKLMNOP presents Admiral Crow and his Amateur Hour. Be sure to phone

[77]

in your votes, folks. The number is Hurry Hill 2000. If the line is busy don't forget to ask for your nickel back. And now . . . Admiral Crow!
(Applause)

CROW   All right, all right. And good evening, friends. Round and round she goes because she's only a hostess on a merry-go-round. Now, who's first tonight? What is your name, young man?

SHRILL   Benedict Shrill.

CROW   What do you do, Benedict?

SHRILL   I'm a steamfitter.

CROW   A steamfitter. You cut up the steam and fit it into Turkish Baths, do you?

SHRILL   No. I work on factory whistles mostly. I put the steam into Thermos bottles. Then I take the Thermos bottle round to the factories.

CROW   And they let the steam loose in the whistles?

SHRILL   Yeah.

CROW   And what are you going to do for us tonight, Benedict?

SHRILL   Nothin'.

CROW   I asked you a civil question.

SHRILL   And I'm givin' you a civil answer. I ain't doin' nothin'.

CROW   Then why are you here at my microphone?

SHRILL   I come up to get your autograph.

CROW   Well, get down out of here.

SHRILL   Not without no applause, I don't get down.

CROW   Hand me that applause card, boy.

[78]

BOY   Here you are, Admiral.

           (Applause)

CROW   All right! All right! *(Phone rings)* Admiral Crow's Amateur Hour . . . Oh yes. Thank you. *(Phone clicks)* Well . . . the first telephone bulletin is in: 400 votes for Trundle Pulp, the Yodeling Taxidermist. Trundle hasn't been on yet. The votes are coming in from California. There's a difference in time, you know. They say the program is coming over beautifully out there. And here's a message from the Governor of the Thousand Islands. They're making me an honorary beachcomber on Island 702. And thanks to Mr. and Mrs. Fumfet of New Orleans for the corn pone recipe.

WOMAN   *(Fades in)* You stand still, Donald. I'll find out.

DONALD   But I gotta go on, Ma.

CROW   You'll have to sit down, Madam, until your name is called.

WOMAN   You've got to put my boy on right away, Admiral.

DONALD   Yeh. I gotta go.

CROW   I haven't mentioned our Honor City yet. The Honor City comes next.

WOMAN   Donald's just going to recite. It won't take a second.

DONALD   The boy stood on the burning deck . . .

           (Gong)

DONALD   What's the big idea?

[79]

WOMAN	Yes. Of all the nerve!
CROW	The boy will recite when I mention the Honor City and not before!
DONALD	But I gotta go, Ma.
CROW	Well, go!
WOMAN	Come, Donald!
CROW	Tonight we salute that quaint old city nestling back in those peaceful hills. The city we all love and venerate: 200 square miles of hail-fellow-well-met. Here the first eye-dropper was made. Here it was that John Bundle jumped out of a window, landed on his rubber heels, and got the idea for the pogo stick. The first hot-dog stand not to charge for its mustard was opened here. Situated on the shores of the second largest lake in America, the home of the biggest dental floss factory in the world . . . we love you. Tonight, we salute . . . Tonight . . . . . Tonight, our Honor City is . . . *(Pause)* Who took that slip of paper? Boy!
BOY	Yes, Admiral?
CROW	Who took that piece of paper from my desk here?
BOY	I don't know, Admiral. I was helping the one-girl band.
CROW	But the Honor City! Who are we saluting? Don't stand there gaping! Get me a vice-president or an aspirin.
BOY	Yes sir.

(Door slams)

CROW   Tonight . . . we salute the city you all know so well. That metropolis that needs no introduction.

(Door opens)

TIMKEN   Admiral! I'm Timken, Vice-President in Charge of No Smoking in the Halls. You sent for a vice-president?

CROW   Yes. This is terrible. Some thief has filched my slip! I don't know the Honor City!

TIMKEN   Oh. This *is* terrible. Is it South Bend?

CROW   No, that's not it.

TIMKEN   Walla Walla?

CROW   No, I've saluted both Wallas. It's only one word. Get me a map.

TIMKEN   Yes sir.

CROW   *(Phone rings)* Yes . . . 300 votes for the Whistling Mousetrap Maker? I can't take any votes now. What will you do with them? Hold them for thirty days. If anybody calls for them, you'll join Unit 23. *(Phone clicks)*

TIMKEN   Here's a map, Admiral. Was it Chillicothe?

CROW   No, I saluted Chillicothe last week. They dedicated a Totem Pole to me.

TIMKEN   What state was the Honor City in?

CROW   How should I know? I'm saluting all over.

TIMKEN   Here's Oklahoma. Enid? Sapulpa? Muskogee?

CROW   No! No! No!

TIMKEN   Nobile, Mississippi?

[81]

CROW   That might be it. Get the Mayor of Nobile on the phone. I'll ask him.

WOMAN   How much longer will Donald have to wait, Admiral?

CROW   Madam, this is no time . . .

WOMAN   He could recite while you're fussin' around.

DONALD   The boy stood on the burning deck . . .

CROW   Shut up, boy!

TIMKEN   The mayor of Nobile on the phone, Admiral.

CROW   I can't ask him if Nobile is the Honor City point-blank. It would be an insult.

TIMKEN   Hint around. Play possum. Here's the phone.

MAYOR   Hello, this is the Mayor of Nobile gassin'. Who is it?

CROW   Admiral Crow.

MAYOR   Are you the guy with the amateurs?

CROW   Yes, yes!

MAYOR   Why didn't you send back that fire helmet?

CROW   Fire helmet?

MAYOR   Yes. We made you Fire Chief for one day and you never returned the helmet. The Chief here is going to fires bare-headed.

CROW   Have I saluted Nobile?

MAYOR   Quit stallin', Admiral. We been honored. Just send back the helmet.

(Phone clicks)

CROW   It wasn't Nobile.

TIMKEN   What about Gloucester, Massachusetts?

CROW   I don't know. Call the City Hall.

QUARTET	*(Sings)* "Hand Me Down My Walking Cane . . ."
CROW	Stop that nasal monkey business! *(Gong sounds)* Who told you hillbillies to sing?
SINGER	We gotta go on, Admiral. Our trailer's outside the studio. Pappy'll get a ticket for parkin'.
CROW	I'm an honorary Chief of Police. I'll fix Pappy's ticket. Sit down.
TIMKEN	Gloucester on the phone, Admiral.
CROW	Hello.
SEC'TRY	City Hall. Mayor's secretary.
CROW	This is Admiral Crow.
SEC'TRY	Oh, yes. I saw your unit at the filling station last week.
CROW	Yes. Has my program saluted Gloucester yet?
SEC'TRY	No.
CROW	Is Gloucester a quaint old city, 200 square miles of hail-fellow-well-met? Was the first hot-dog stand not to charge for mustard started there?
SEC'TRY	No, Gloucester's the home of the first fishball.
CROW	No, no! Hang up. *(Phone clicks)* It's not Gloucester. This is exasperating. *(Phone rings)* Yes? You have 300 votes for the Whistling Mousetrap Maker? I know, you told me that. No. Go away. *(Phone clicks)*
TIMKEN	Here's another one, Admiral. Cornhusk, Maryland.
CROW	Call them up. . . . Do something, Timken.
WOMAN	Are you ready for Donald now, Admiral?

DONALD	Yeah, what about my recitation, Big Belly?
CROW	Why, you ragamuffin . . .
WOMAN	Who you callin' ragamuffin, Sponge-nose?
DONALD	Tell him, Ma. Pin his ears back.
CROW	Isn't there enough trouble on this program?
WOMAN	You don't know what trouble is yet. Hold my bridgework, Donald.
TIMKEN	Excuse my butting in. Cornhusk, Maryland on the phone.
CROW	Hello, this is Admiral Crow.
MAYOR	Mayor of Cornhusk speaking. What's up. Have ye lost a unit?
CROW	No. Have I saluted Cornhusk on my program?
MAYOR	Not yet. Yer shootin' off about us two weeks from tonight.
CROW	Could you fill in as the Honor City tonight?
MAYOR	Not on such short notice. The Chamber of Commerce is up to New York auditioning for a Community Sing.
CROW	All right. Good-by. *(Phone clicks)* Where's that vice-president? Timken!
TIMKEN	I'm here biting my nails, Admiral.
CROW	This is no time for gluttony, Timken. Haven't you found another city? *(Phone rings)* Yes . . . 300 votes for the Whistling Mousetrap Maker? Oh, my! *(Phone clicks)* Oh, this is upsetting. I'll be disgraced.
WOMAN	You'll be disgraced. What about Donald and me: we'll be decrepit.

[84]

DONALD   Yeah. Does the boy get on the burnin' deck, or don't he?

CROW   I've told you two for the last time!

WOMAN   And I'm tellin' you for the last time, Gollywog. Wait till we get home. Andiron, New Jersey, won't take this layin' down.

DONALD   Oh boy! The Loyal Order of Moose'll be off your program for life.

CROW   What has Andiron to do with my amateur program?

WOMAN   Tonight's Andiron Night!

DONALD   Yeah. And I'm here to recite. The Moose sent me. I got 8000 phone calls pledged.

CROW   Andiron, New Jersey! That name does sound familiar!

DONALD   It oughta. You had it written down on this slip on your desk.

WOMAN   Give him back his slip, Donald.

CROW   Andiron! MY HONOR CITY!

WOMAN   That's what we been tryin' to tell you.

DONALD   Now do I recite?

CROW   Yes, Son. Tonight, folks, our Honor City is Andiron, New Jersey. And the favorite son of Andiron is sitting right here on my lap. What's your name, Sonny Boy?

DONALD   Donald Thompson.

CROW   Donald Thompson is right here on my knee, waiting to recite.

WOMAN   Clear your throat, Donald.

[85]

DONALD   *(Clears throat)* The boy stood on the burning deck . . .

ORCHESTRA   *(Up to finish)*

Town Hall Tonight began to pay dividends on the work we had invested in it. The program's popularity continued to grow. Suddenly Town Hall Tonight became the Fred Allen Show. Why a distinctive title that had proved its appeal should be abandoned is difficult to understand unless you have been exposed to the workings of the alleged mind of a certain type of dynamic advertising executive.

Along the hectic way we had changed advertising agencies. The agency with whom we had originally started, the man who had helped himself to our program format, was servicing two dentifrice accounts — Ipana, our product, and Colgate, which shall be nameless. Both toothpastes sponsored radio programs. Our Ipana and Sal Hepatica show had a higher rating, which fomented some concern in Colgate circles. These circles, following a cluster of conferences, an exchange of memos and clichés — "seeing eye to eye," "being sold to the hilt," and "mother-henning it for a while" — crystallized their thinking. Looking into the crystal ball, those who did look into it saw a message reading "No advertising agency can divide its loyalty between two similar products." Shortly after, Colgate issued a soapy ultimatum. The agency would have to give up one of the toothpaste accounts. The choice was not too difficult to make: the Colgate advertising budget was $4,000,000; the Ipana budget was $1,000,000. Our program, lock, stock and stooges, was moved to another advertising concern.

The president of the new agency had been a famous quarterback in college football. An old wives' tale often told around the watercooler in the office related that, after he had left college, whenever he met one of the other players who had been on the team with him he could never recognize the fellow until he had asked him to bend over. The president was going through life as a quarterback running the team. He also did some of his thinking at the quarterback's working level. Only two people think lower than a quarterback — a sandhog on the job and a man looking out of a manhole.

When our Town Hall Tonight program was taken over by the new agency things began to happen — mostly to us. The college quarterback started sending turtle-necked memos which intimated that, as the mink said when it backed into the electric fan, "the fur is going to fly." The show was going to receive "All of the agency's thinking," which meant that everything we were doing was going to be overhauled completely. We were told that the Town Hall idea was corny. The most popular show in radio at that time was Jack Benny's. Jack had a group of pleasant people gathered around the microphone to engage in an informal half-hour of comedy, music and song. The quarterback, being an advertising man, knew the importance of the word "copy." His solution was that all we needed to improve our show was to copy the Benny program in style and structure.

I tried to explain the value of the Town Hall title and the appeal the locale had to small-town listeners. He said that the Jack Benny-type show was the trend. I argued that no two comedians could use the same methods. A comedian can only be funny doing and saying the things that fit his personality and feel right to him. The quarterback's reply bluntly stated that Jack Benny's show had the largest audience on any network. The size of our audience could be improved. My rejoinder asserted that no one person can please everybody. Heinz made 57 varieties of pickles yet he did not please all of the pickle lovers. Other people made pickles and survived in business. I claimed that radio was like the pickle business. Let Jack Benny go along selling his big dill. I would take the other side of the street and peddle my little gherkins. It was as futile as trying to convince a Russian delegate at the U.N. Nothing helped. The Town Hall title disappeared. We became just another group of actors gathered around a microphone in a radio studio. The colorful illusion had been completely stripped from the program.

The one ingredient we did rescue from debacle was the presentation of the News. The form was retained. Only the title was changed — instead of the Town Hall News the audience now heard the March of Trivia:

The March of Trivia

ALLEN — Worst fog in New York history blankets city for four days, slowing down highway traffic, endangering navigation, and causing airlines to cancel hundreds of flights. Density of fog is confirmed by flashes received from Metropolitan area and Eastern Seaboard towns. Report from Portland, Maine, states . . .

VOICE   Fog here so thick folks had to tread fog to get where they was goin'.

ALLEN   At New Rochelle, New York . . .

RUBE   Fog here was terrible. Birds flyin' south were carryin' glowworms in their beaks so they could see where they were goin'.

ALLEN   Corn Cob, Vermont, flashes . . .

OLD MAN   Fog here got so bad you couldn't see nawthin'. Ain't nawthin to see, nohow!

ALLEN   To check on effects of fog in the New York area, the March of Trivia interviews a downtown housewife who enjoyed a freak adventure in the heavy fog, Mrs. Maxine Messbaum. You had an unusual experience, Mrs. Messbaum?

MRS. MESSBAUM   Unusual? This is puttink it mildly.

ALLEN   What happened?

MRS. MESSBAUM   Where I am livink is a ground floor. Upstairs is a tenement.

ALLEN   I see.

MRS. MESSBAUM   All day long my husband, Cicero, is away woikink.

ALLEN   Cicero Messbaum. Your husband was named after the great Roman orator?

[92]

MRS. MESSBAUM   No. Cicero is a street in Brooklyn.

ALLEN   I see. You say you live on the ground floor?

MRS. MESSBAUM   Exactel. When I am goink by the A and P always I am steppink out the window and I am already on the street.

ALLEN   You never use the door?

MRS. MESSBAUM   Always the window.

ALLEN   Fine.

MRS. MESSBAUM   Comink back, I am steppink in the window. Presto! I am home.

ALLEN   Well, what happened?

MRS. MESSBAUM   Tuesday it's a fog. I am steppink out the window. And goink to buy dinner.

ALLEN   The fog was bad.

MRS. MESSBAUM   It could be Pittsburg. So walkink along I am feelink buildings.

ALLEN   How did you find the store?

MRS. MESSBAUM   It is a delicatessen, I am smellink.

ALLEN   You made your purchase?

MRS. MESSBAUM   I am buyink two pounds cold cuts. On Tuesdays Cicero is likink cold cuts.

ALLEN   A gourmet.

MRS. MESSBAUM   Every time.

ALLEN   After buying the cold cuts did you start right home, Mrs. Messbaum?

MRS. MESSBAUM   Creepink but with feelink I am comink to the open window. I am steppink in the window. I am home.

[93]

ALLEN	And then?
MRS. MESSBAUM	I am fixink hup the cold cuts and sittink down to wait for Cicero. Suddenly it is happenink.
ALLEN	What?
MRS. MESSBAUM	A man is steppink in the window. I am cominik from behind and kissink him. He is toinink around.
ALLEN	And?
MRS. MESSBAUM	It is not Cicero.
ALLEN	Not Cicero? You mean you were in the wrong apartment?
MRS. MESSBAUM	It is so foggy I am steppink in a window two blocks down.
ALLEN	What happened?
MRS. MESSBAUM	Luckily, the stranger is likink cold cuts. We are eatink dinner.
ALLEN	But what became of Cicero?
MRS. MESSBAUM	Who knows? Next week, I am no longer Mrs. Cicero Messbaum.
ALLEN	No?
MRS. MESSBAUM	I am Mrs. Pierpont Weintraub, M.D.
ALLEN	Congratulations, Mrs. Pierpont Weintraub, as you start life anew two blocks down.

The Sixth Avenue El

ALLEN	New York City, New York. After 60 years of continuous service, the Sixth Avenue Elevated Lines ceased operations at midnight, Sunday.

Title of entire elevated structure passes to the city for $3,500,000, and work of demolition will begin at once. Town Hall News interviews native New Yorkers, young and old, to get opinions on the passing of this historic landmark. First, Mr. Bismark Tort, attorney for the stockholders. . . . What caused the El's downfall, Mr. Tort?

MR. TORT   The trend has been down. When the trend is down the subways get the business.

ALLEN   I see. Are you taking any legal action for the elevated, Mr. Tort?

MR. TORT   We're taking the Sixth Avenue El into court.

ALLEN   It will be quite a job, won't it?

MR. TORT   Yes. But I think we can get it in in sections.

ALLEN   You feel you have grounds for a suit, Mr. Tort?

MR. TORT   Unquestionably. In 1903 we signed a lease for 999 years.

ALLEN   Hasn't the city made you an offer to settle?

MR. TORT   Yes. They want to give us the World's Fair when they're through with it.

ALLEN   Well . . . I hope everything will come out all right, Mr. Tort.

MR. TORT   It will. All's El that Ends El . . . That's Shakespeare.

ALLEN	Oh . . . I thought the mayor was taking it down.
MR. TORT	He is. He got the idea from Shakespeare. That is *sub rosa*.
ALLEN	I have heard nothing, Mr. Tort.
MR. TORT	Too bad. You should have told me. I'd have raised my voice.
ALLEN	If I don't see you, again . . . Merry Christmas, Mr. Tort.
MR. TORT	On Sixth Avenue it's Happy No-El.
ALLEN	A Sixth Avenue housewife who doesn't know what she'll do is Mrs. Elaine O'Gatty.
MRS. O'GATTY	I'm sure gonna miss the old El all right.
ALLEN	Have you been living on Sixth Avenue long, Mrs. O'Gatty?
MRS. O'GATTY	Thoity years. I spent me honeymoon on the Staten Island Ferry. After that we was "at home" on Sixth Avenue.
ALLEN	You've been there a long time.
MRS. O'GATTY	Thoity years, mornin', noon, and night . . . I been hearin' them stratosphere gondolas go by.
ALLEN	Has stopping the trains bothered you and Mr. O'Gatty any?
MRS. O'GATTY	Yeah. The lack o' noise is somethin' brutal. Every midnight a train's been goin' by for 30 years.
ALLEN	Yes.
MRS. O'GATTY	Monday midnight nothin' went by. My old

man jumps up in bed and says, "What's that?"

ALLEN   I guess losing the El is going to take the romance out of your life, Mrs. O'Gatty.

MRS. O'GATTY   I got a lump here, mister.

ALLEN   That bulge in your throat. . . .

MRS. O'GATTY   No. That's me Adam's apple. I got a lump yer can't see. I guess it's sediment.

ALLEN   You're going to miss those old trains passing your flat.

MRS. O'GATTY   Yeah. Thoity years seein' people's profiles. Wise guys throwin' cigarette butts in me window. Wavin' at the motorman. Stickin' me tongue out at dames dressed up.

ALLEN   Yes. It must be an awful blow.

MRS. O'GATTY   Yeah. I wouldn't be surprised if it broke up me home.

ALLEN   Why?

MRS. O'GATTY   Well, me old man woiks down at the Fulton Fish Market. He's the conjunction man.

ALLEN   Conjunction man in a fish market.

MRS. O'GATTY   Yea. His foim makes nothin' but finn and haddie signs. He puts in the conjunction.

ALLEN   But the Sixth Avenue El . . . ?

MRS. O'GATTY   I'm comin' to that. Every Saturday night me old man gets plastered downtown. The bartender lugs him over to the Sixth Avenue El . . .

ALLEN   And puts him on a train.

[97]

MRS. O'GATTY   Carries him on, mister. He's stiff.

ALLEN   What happens?

MRS. O'GATTY   When the train pulls in to Twenty-thoid Street, the conductor rolls him down the stairs into me arms . . . He's home.

ALLEN   What will you do next Saturday night?

MRS. O'GATTY   The subway guard can't roll him up the stairs. I'll be waitin' there to carry him home.

ALLEN   Are you strong enough to lift that load?

MRS. O'GATTY   I'll just carry me husband. He'll be carrying the load.

ALLEN   Thank you. . . . New York's oldest inhabitant has his say about the El: Grandpa Creep.

OLD MAN   I said, "She won't last." When I seen the El goin' up in '78 . . . I said, "She won't last." Well, it only goes to show . . .

ALLEN   To show what, Gramp?

OLD MAN   If ye live long enough, nothin' won't last.

ALLEN   Have you lived in New York all your life?

OLD MAN   Not yet, no. I been here 90 years.

ALLEN   I guess you've seen many changes in the city.

OLD MAN   Lord, yes. I remember Al Smith way back before his derby faded.

ALLEN   You don't say.

OLD MAN   I can remember the Aquarium when it was nothin' but a room full of bait.

ALLEN   That's going back.

OLD MAN   I can remember Tammany Hall when 'twarn't

	nothin' but a Democrat hidin' in a doorway.
ALLEN	And you . . .
OLD MAN	I says, "They won't last." And they ain't, have they?
ALLEN	No.
OLD MAN	It's like I say. Ef ye live long enough, nothin' won't last.
ALLEN	Isn't there anything in New York that *will* last, Gramp?
OLD MAN	Just one thing, son.
ALLEN	What?
OLD MAN	That show, *Tobacco Road*.
ALLEN	Why do you think *Tobacco Road* will last forever?
OLD MAN	Tobacco's habit-formin'.
ALLEN	What are you going to use now that the Sixth Avenue El is down, Gramp?
OLD MAN	Nothin', son. I ain't goin' no place.
ALLEN	Aren't we all . . . and thank you, Grandpa Creep.

Closing Night at The World's Fair

ALLEN Flushing, Long Island. As lights go out on closing night of New York World's Fair, wrecking crews start razing Fair-owned and exhibitors' structures. Newspapers brim with glowing accounts of executives' activities during Fair's two-year run. But what about the unsung heroes of the New York World's Fair? Tonight, the March of Trivia interviews the little

[99]

fellows to get unimportant sidelights on uninteresting data. First, a young lady who welcomed the closing night, Miss Mona Griffin. What did you do at the Fair, Mona?

MONA   I was an Ackabelle.

ALLEN   An Ackabelle?

MONA   Yeah. In the Ackacade.

ALLEN   Ackacade?

MONA   Billy Rose's streamlined swimmin' hole.

ALLEN   How long have you been swimming?

MONA   Since a kid. My mother used to throw me in at Coney Island.

ALLEN   And you'd swim.

MONA   Like a prawn. Everybody used to say, "Look at Mona. She's swimmin' like a prawn."

ALLEN   And that started you on your career?

MONA   Well, first I won a beauty contest.

ALLEN   Where?

MONA   At the Fulton Fish Market. I was Miss Anchovy for 1937.

ALLEN   Miss Anchovy. Then came fame and glory.

MONA   And Billy Rose.

ALLEN   What happened?

MONA   I see an ad "Girls wanted for Ackacade. Must float and have poisonality."

ALLEN   And P.S.: You got the job.

MONA   Yeah. I seen Billy Rose. He says, "I gotta have twenty nynphs." I says, "What's a nynph?" He says, "It's like a pixie, only yer wet."

ALLEN   And you've been in the Aquacade ever since.

MONA   Yeah. I was in five numbers doin' four shows a day.

ALLEN   Did you enjoy your work, Mona?

MONA   I didn't mind it at first. Then my hair started looking like watercress.

ALLEN   Really?

ALLEN   The next thing I know my arms is stickin' to my side like fins.

ALLEN   You don't say.

MONA   Every time I sit down I can't get up.

ALLEN   You mean . . .

MONA   Yeah. Barnacles.

ALLEN   You were waterlogged.

MONA   I can't take a step I squish. If I stand still I leave puddles.

ALLEN   You poor thing.

MONA   I can't sleep. I'm tossin' in the bed treadin' mattress.

ALLEN   I guess you're glad the Fair is closed.

MONA   Yeah. But it's gonna be a struggle tryna live outta water.

ALLEN   Have you got another job?

MONA   Yeah. I'm dancin' in a nightclub over in Joisey.

ALLEN   Do you think you'll miss the Aquacade?

MONA   Na. This joint's a dive. I'm sittin' pretty.

When World War II started, the complexion of the news items on our show changed greatly. In the early days of the war after Pearl Harbor the papers were filled with depressing news. Some weeks it was impossible for us to find subject matter that could be treated in a comedy manner.

As the war progressed the Government instituted rationing. Food, rubber, gasoline and other shortages were serious. During these days we used our news reels to reflect the reactions of the average man to the various obstacles that the war and the government were placing in the path of his normal progress and everyday existence.

The comedy dialogue had to be written carefully. While trying to get laughs we had to be serious in the treatment of the matter being discussed and stress its importance to all of us in the country. These liberties taken with the news must have gotten results. During the war years, we received letters from Mayor LaGuardia, of New York City, Leon Henderson, head of the O.P.A., and many other government agency heads complimenting us for calling government drives and other information to the attention of the mass audience. Mayor LaGuardia once told me, during the water shortage in New York City, that our program had been able to reach more people in one hour, and make them conscious of the City's plight and tell them how they could help, than the City had been able to do through its normal channels in several days.

One of our news reels on the "Dim-out" reached the country's ears in this form:

ALLEN   New York City, New York. New dim-out order, to curtail haze of light thrown on water by city's illumination, vitally affects apartment dwellers and store owners. The March of Trivia interviews several specimens of riffraff to learn their strange experiences since new dim-out rule went into effect. First, a real Broadway character. What is your name again, Brother?

SHERMAN The hep set calls me Sharp Sherman.

ALLEN What is your work?

SHERMAN Work is a sucker's pastime, chum. I live by my wits. There's one born every minute. Somebody's gotta take 'em. That's where I come in. Sharp Sherman.

ALLEN How do you get by?

SHERMAN Rackets, chum. I keep 'em up to the minute.

ALLEN You're a smart operator, eh?

SHERMAN Who was the first one on Broadway to sell them postcards: "Don't open 'em, Men, till you get 'em home"? Who started paintin' Brussels sprouts with white enamel and sellin' 'm for gardenias? Sharp Sherman, chum. I don't miss a trick.

ALLEN What about this dim-out, Sherman?

SHERMAN I got a coupla gimmicks operatin' already, Chum.

ALLEN What gimmicks?

SHERMAN I got a dim-out Racin' Form.

ALLEN What is that?

SHERMAN Hundreds of horseplayers used to stand in front of restaurants and read their Racin' Forms by the light of the restaurant windows. Today, them windows is dimmed out.

[103]

ALLEN   Oh. And your —

SHERMAN   My Racin' Form's got a lightnin' bug tied on it. A horseplayer can read it anyplace.

ALLEN   What is your other dim-out gimmick?

SHERMAN   I'm light-leggin'.

ALLEN   What is light-legging?

SHERMAN   It's like bootleggin' only with a light. Durin' a dim-out you can't see nothin'. Yer afraid to strike a match. A cop might be around. I nudge you and say, "Can you use a little light, chum?"

ALLEN   What would I need light for?

SHERMAN   Suppose you're goin' in the Automat. I foller you in, whip out a piece of Neon and light up the slots for you. Somebody says hello to you on the street. You don't know who it is. I light 'em up for you.

ALLEN   Tell me, Sharp Sherman, what do you charge for this service?

SHERMAN   I take a chance.

ALLEN   How do you mean?

SHERMAN   I put out my Neon. . . .

ALLEN   Yes.

SHERMAN   And you pay me off in the dark.

ALLEN   A man who is paid in the dark can't make light of his salary. And thank you, Sharp Sherman.

During the coffee shortage we reported the reactions of the coffee lovers of the nation to their dilemma. At Christmas, I had some individual coffee beans wrapped by Cartier in jewel boxes and mailed out as Xmas tokens. One coffee bean was mailed to the White House. A few days later we received this acknowledgment:

THE WHITE HOUSE
WASHINGTON
December 28, 1942

Personal

DEAR FRED ALLEN:

You and your wife, more than all others, must be held responsible for my continuance in the White House. During the past anguished months, with their coffeeless breakfasts, I had decided to resign as Commander in chief and had been offered an appointment as Sergeant Major in the army with the promise that I would be stationed at one of the bases in Brazil where I could have coffee six times a day.

Today, all is changed. Your coffee bean has made the sun come out. Under my new patented process I find that I can grind it and percolate it twice a day for at least three months. If you really want to accomplish the heart's objective of some of your fellow radio commentators, you can force me out of the White House in ninety days by not sending me another coffee bean! On the other hand, if you do not think I am as big a bad wolf as they paint me, send me another bean the end of March.

With all good wishes for the new year,

Very sincerely yours,

(signed) FRANKLIN D. ROOSEVELT

Radio was booming. The networks had clients waiting in line to buy time. Under pressure the hour programs began to disappear. The trend was to the half-hour show. This accomplished several things. It enabled the advertiser to economize on his radio time costs and still get the same selling results with concentrated commercial copy. It enabled the networks to accommodate more customers.

Typical of these new shows were the quiz and audience-participation programs. They became popular with the sponsors long before the listeners at home were conditioned to them. These shows appealed to the businessman because they were cheap.

Reduced to essentials, a quiz show required one master of ceremonies, preferably with prominent teeth, two underpaid girls to do research and supply the quiz questions and a small herd of morons, stampeded in the studio audience and rounded up at the microphone to compete for prizes. The prizes generally were watches, washing machines or electrical gadgets which were donated by their makers in return for a mention of their merchandise on the program.

The audience-participation show varied slightly. This pseudo-entertainment consisted of a covey of frowsy housewives, flushed at a neighborhood supermarket, and an assortment of tottering male extroverts gathered from park benches. The purpose of the program was to establish the senility of the participants in the process of playing an antiquated parlor game. These shows not only were inexpensive — some of them became very popular, which justified their existence in advertising and corporate circles.

Late that spring the Bristol-Myers Company asked us if we could do our show in thirty minutes. We could, but since we had already issued cast, writers' and musicians' contracts on a full hour basis we had to continue the hour operation for an additional year.

[106]

At this point the Texas Company took over the program and the Fred Allen Show now became The Texaco Star Theater. Our budget was increased and we were at last able to book guests on a regular basis. We were still trying to find ideas that could be sustained over a period of weeks. There was a rumor that vaudeville was coming back. We ran a series of interviews with prominent actors to obtain their reactions to the news.

The Bert Wheeler and Georgie Jessel routines came out this way:

Vaudeville with Bert Wheeler

ALLEN	Your face looks familiar.
BERT	You remember me. I played on the bill with you in vaudeville.
ALLEN	In vaudeville?
BERT	At the Lyric in Glen Falls, remember? The manager was a midget. When he paid off, the actors had to kneel down so he could hand them the money.
ALLEN	You say this was the Lyric?
BERT	You remember the little orchestra. The drummer had no arms. He used to butt the drum with his head.
ALLEN	Who was on the bill?
BERT	There was Corrigan and his calculating catfish.
ALLEN	The catfish was in a big glass tank. Corrigan would say "How many days in the week?" and the catfish would blow seven bubbles.

BERT That's right. For the finish of the act, Corrigan had a Red Herring, a Whitefish and a Bluefish make like the American flag.

ALLEN With forty-eight starfish. What a finish! An inkfish would write out *God Bless America*. Whatever became of Corrigan?

BERT The catfish got amnesia. He couldn't remember the routine.

ALLEN Gosh, that's too bad.

BERT The last time I saw Corrigan he was playing the smalltime with a sardine.

ALLEN That was some show.

BERT The great La Flemme, the Fire-eater, was on the bill.

ALLEN La Flemme was a million laughs. He'd go into a restaurant, order a crepe suzette, eat the flame and get up and leave the crepe suzette.

BERT I saw the great La Flemme last week. Things are tough.

ALLEN No kidding.

BERT La Flemme is around snapping at hotfoots.

ALLEN Glen Falls . . . Didn't we live at Mother Mulcahy's Boardinghouse?

BERT There was a big sign outside. It said: MARTHA WASHINGTON SLEPT HERE.

ALLEN Do you think Martha Washington really slept there?

BERT She must have. The first morning I woke up two gumdrops were in bed with me.

[108]

ALLEN   Remember those meals at Mother Mulcahy's?

BERT   The breast of veal had a sweater on it.

ALLEN   Mother Mulcahy used to serve the biggest steak
            in town. It had horns on it. While you were eat-
            ing your steak you could hang your hat on it.
            And the rates — room and board, a dollar a day.

BERT   If you had ulcers, it was 75 cents a day.

ALLEN   Yes. It all comes back to me now. . . . So you're
            little Bert Wheeler?

BERT   Yes. What about this job, Fred?

ALLEN   We need a comedian who is funny — who can
            sing and do dramatic acting.

BERT   When do I go to work, Fred?

ALLEN   Not so fast, Bert. You have to audition first.

BERT   Why don't you come over to the Copacabaña and
            see me work?

ALLEN   The Copa is a nightclub. This is for radio. You
            have to keep it clean.

BERT   I've never told a joke on the stage that I wouldn't
            tell in front of my Mother.

ALLEN   Where is your Mother?

BERT   She's with a burlesque show.

ALLEN   Fine. What are some of your jokes?

BERT   Coca-Cola was on my mind . . . all day today.

ALLEN   Why Coca-Cola?

BERT   On Father's Day I always think of Pop.

ALLEN   I see.

BERT   My girl feeds her cat lemons. Has she got a sour
            puss!

ALLEN   How about telling one of your gags to give me an idea of your radio delivery.

BERT   I can tell a very quick joke. It will give you an idea of what kind of a comedian I am. I'll say to you "I just bought a dog," and you say to me, "Does your dog chase rats?"

ALLEN   Is that all I say?

BERT   Yeah, that's all you say. Why?

ALLEN   It isn't much for me to look forward to, is it?

BERT   Yeah. But this happens to be my joke. Isn't this part big enough for you?

ALLEN   Well, actually, it isn't the size of the part. In the first place I don't care whether your dog chases rats, or not. If your dog chases rats you should send him to a psychiatrist. He may have a rodent neurosis. A psychiatrist can get through to the dog's subconscious and make a new man of your dog.

BERT   You're making a Federal case out of one joke. Don't you want to do it?

ALLEN   All right. *(Glumly)* Does your dog chase rats?

BERT   It's no good that way. I'll never get a laugh on it.

ALLEN   Can you do it any better?

BERT   Certainly I can.

ALLEN   Let me hear you.

BERT   Does your dog chase rats?

ALLEN   Start running and you'll find out. Well, that takes care of the jokes, Bert.

[110]

Belles Lettres With George Jessel

PORTLAND   Who are we having as our guest tonight?

ALLEN   Portland! It's "*Whom* are we having as our guest?" Our guest is a great author. If he hears a grammatical error he'll swoon. This man is an English perfectionist.

PORTLAND   And he's a great author?

ALLEN   Yes. This gentleman only recently entered the field of literature. He has written a great book. Our guest is George Jessel; his autobiography, *So Help Me,* has just been published.

PORTLAND   George Jessel wrote a book?

ALLEN   That's why I want to see him tonight. I'm going to write the story of my life and Jessel can help me.

PORTLAND   But how can you write your life when you haven't finished living it, yet?

ALLEN   Jessel will know what to do. He isn't dead yet and he wrote his life. Maybe on the last page of my book I can put To be Continued. Then I can send —

(Knock at door)

ALLEN   Come in!

(Door opens)

ALLEN   Georgie Jessel!

(Applause)

GEORGE   Thank you. Good evening, Ladies and Gentlemen. Tonight, the world's my oyster. Which I with sword will open. Shakespeare's *Merry Wives of Windsor*. Act Two. Scene Two.

ALLEN   Georgie, I greet you not only as a friend, but I rejoice that you have finally found your place in the field of letters. It is George Jessel, the writer — the Svengali of the Phrase — we welcome to our humble midst this night.

GEORGE   Fred! Two split infinitives and a dangling metaphor.

ALLEN   I'm sorry, Georgie.

GEORGE   People will think this is Duffy's Tavern.

ALLEN   I'll watch my grammar, Georgie.

GEORGE   Please do.

ALLEN   Gosh, Georgie. When I see you with that monocle in your eye, and think that you used to be just Jessel, the actor . . .

GEORGE   My pantaloon days are over, Fred. The grease paint on my collar is just a hazy memory.

ALLEN   Yes. Now, you're Mr. Jessel, the author. You're even starting to look like an author.

GEORGE   Yes. I'm letting my hair grow long. With me this is not so easy.

ALLEN   Why do you wear the monocle, Georgie?

GEORGE   Only one eye is weak. Why should I wear glasses?

ALLEN   But the other eye . . .

GEORGE   When the other eye goes bad, I'll get another monocle.

ALLEN   You've certainly changed. I don't see you in Lindy's any more.

GEORGE   No. I go to a little teashop downtown. The in-
              telligentsia eats there. We have a community
              teabag. If you come after six o'clock the tea is
              weak.

ALLEN   Did you move out of that actor's hotel on 46th
              Street?

GEORGE   Yes. I'm living in an attic down in Greenwich Vil-
              lage. In the Village everybody writes. Why, only
              yesterday Hemingway showed me his new book.

ALLEN   Ernest Hemingway?

GEORGE   No. This is Sam Hemingway. He's a butcher. He
              can't get any meat so he writes.

ALLEN   Oh.

GEORGE   Sam's new book is *Mission to a Black Market*.

ALLEN   But, tell me, Georgie, isn't this literary life a let-
              down?

GEORGE   Letdown? Since my autobiography, *So Help Me*,
              came out, believe me, I've been on the go, as
              Milton once so aptly put it.

ALLEN   You're rushed, eh?

GEORGE   Every morning I'm in Brentano's basement auto-
              graphing. Then I rush around to booklovers'
              meetings lecturing.

ALLEN   I see.

GEORGE   Every noon I'm at the Authors' League Cafeteria.

ALLEN   Selling your book.

GEORGE   With the forty-cent lunch I come to your table
              and read a chapter. If you're eating soup I read
              through a megaphone.

[113   ]

ALLEN   You are busy.

GEORGE   On top of that they asked me to join the Book of
          the Month Club. I refused.

ALLEN   Why?

GEORGE   Who can write a book every month?

ALLEN   Who do they think you are, Henry Kaiser?

GEORGE   I told them. A boat you can leave portholes in.
          A book has got to be solid all the way through.

ALLEN   Tell me, Georgie, how did you come to write
          the story of your life?

GEORGE   Well, one day I went down to the Draft Board.
          The man said, "How did you get to look like this
          in only thirty-seven years?" That set me think-
          ing.

ALLEN   I see.

GEORGE   I started thinking back. My grandfather with the
          long beard. My grandfather had the longest
          beard in the Bronx. It had buttons down the
          front and a belt in the back.

ALLEN   Gosh.

GEORGE   I thought about my Uncle Louie, the Sturgeon
          King. Louie was crazy. All day long he used to
          sit playing gin rummy.

ALLEN   How did you know Louie was crazy?

GEORGE   He played gin rummy with no cards. . . . I
          thought of my first love.

ALLEN   Love, eh?

GEORGE   Yes, Fred. Love like spinach is highly overrated.

ALLEN   What about marriage?

[114   ]

GEORGE   Marriage is a mistake every man should make.
          . . . I thought about my father. Every day, he sat
          on the front steps in his bathrobe wearing a fez.

ALLEN   That's all he did for a living — wear a fez?

GEORGE   No. At night my father would put on his dress
          suit and high silk hat. And I'd run after him down
          the street laughing.

ALLEN   Laughing at your own father?

GEORGE   Yes. His shirtfront used to light up and spell
          Flugleman's Roumanian Restaurant. My father
          had a big chest.

ALLEN   You must have had some pleasant memories,
          Georgie.

GEORGE   Yes, Fred. When I had emptied the top drawer of
          my mind, I had a book.

ALLEN   That's what I'm going to do, Georgie. I'm going
          to write the story of my life. If you can help me —

GEORGE   Authors get big money, Fred.

ALLEN   I'll pay you. But I've got to make sure. How is
          your book doing?

GEORGE   Believe me, Fred. The way people are buying my
          book you'd think it showed how to make gasoline
          out of Coca-Cola. In Union Square it's outselling
          PM.

ALLEN   How did the critics —

GEORGE   I've been carrying the reviews in my hand since
          the book came out. I have them right here. Listen
          to these. The *Hoboken Herald:* "Jessel is a new
          shining light on the literary horizon." The *Bronx*

[115]

Bugle: "Epis and Epic." The *Weehawken Gazette:* "Dynamite in every page." The *Staten Island Chronicle:* "A *must* on your reading list." The *New York Times* — Ach! Who reads the *Times.*

ALLEN   But the critics had to read your book Georgie. Who else is —

GEORGE   Everybody is reading my book.

ALLEN   Not everybody.

GEORGE   Oh, no? You have a thousand people here in the studio. I'll pick any one at random. This lady in the second row. Madam, will you step up here, please.

ALLEN   Look, Georgie, we can't interrupt a radio broadcast.

GEORGE   Radio, schmadio. I want to prove something. Will you step over this way, Madam —

ALLEN   My name is Allen, Madam. This is Mr. Jessel.

WOMAN   I'm glad to know you both.

GEORGE   Madam, I just want to ask you one question. Have you read a book called *So Help Me,* written by George Jessel?

WOMAN   *So Help Me?*

GEORGE   If you haven't read it, say so. Mr. Allen and I just want the truth.

WOMAN   I have read the book.

GEORGE   You see, Fred. I picked a stranger at random. This lady has read my book. Thank you, Madam, I'm very —

[116]

ALLEN	Just a minute, Madam.
WOMAN	Yes, Mr. Allen.
ALLEN	Madam, what do you think of the book?
WOMAN	I think it is the greatest book I ever read. I think that Mr. Jessel will go down in history as one of this country's greatest geniuses.
GEORGE	Madam, I'm deeply indebted to you for that statement. Allow me to help you to your seat.
ALLEN	One moment, Madam. Will you tell me your name?
WOMAN	I'm Mrs. Jessel.
ALLEN	This gentleman's mother?
WOMAN	Yes, sir.
ALLEN	A stranger picked at random, eh Georgie?
GEORGE	It's a coincidence, Fred.
ALLEN	A coincidence.
GEORGE	A thing like this couldn't happen again in a thousand years.
WOMAN	Did I say what you told me, Georgie?
GEORGE	Yes, Mama. Just like I told you. You were a sweetheart.
WOMAN	Don't stay out too late, Georgie.
GEORGE	I won't. Now run home, Mama. This program may need some jokes later. I might have to telephone you.
WOMAN	Good-by.
ALLEN	Good-by, Mrs. Jessel.
GEORGE	I know what you're thinking, Fred.
ALLEN	I hope so!

[117]

GEORGE   But don't worry. My mother's appearance to-
          night is free. I told her it's a benefit.

ALLEN   I wasn't worrying about that. I was just thinking
          of who else I can get to write my biography.

GEORGE   Fred, as a friend, believe me. My book is a suc-
          cess. They even want it for a movie: *The Life of
          George Jessel.*

ALLEN   *The Life of George Jessel.* Who can play it? Don
          Ameche doesn't look anything like you.

GEORGE   With makeup they can make him look younger.
          Let me write your life's story, Fred.

ALLEN   Well, I don't . . .

GEORGE   If you've been leading a double life, I can write
          it in two volumes.

ALLEN   Well, all right.

GEORGE   I'll take some notes. Give me the facts.

ALLEN   I was born in Boston in a three-family house, on
          the first floor.

GEORGE   That's no good. A biography has got to have
          color. The names must be important. A three-
          family house — who knows what is in the bot-
          tom deck of a three-decker sandwich?

ALLEN   But. I —

GEORGE   Here's how we begin. You were born in a log
          cabin. Your father was a poor rail-splitter.

ALLEN   But my father —

GEORGE   We don't come right out and say your father was
          Abraham Lincoln. But we keep referring to him
          as "Honest Abe."

[118]

ALLEN	"Honest Abe" Allen.
GEORGE	Your Mother was one of the Hanks Girls.
ALLEN	Fine. . . .
GEORGE	What happened during your childhood?
ALLEN	I played with two kids, Bung-eye Healy and Finky Mallard.
GEORGE	Bung-eye Healy is out. This is what we say: "Allen's boyhood was a happy one. Playing leap-frog with General Grant. Duck-on-the-rock with Patrick Henry. And when Tory bullies picked on little Benjamin Franklin — who beat them off?
ALLEN	Who?
GEORGE	You, the fearless Freddy Allen. Among his other friends one little boy had a pony. This was later Paul Revere.
ALLEN	But, Georgie, my friends —
GEORGE	Who knows your friends — you and the F.B.I., maybe. Go on with your life, Fred.
ALLEN	Well, I worked in the Boston Library, then I got a job helping to dam the Charles River.
GEORGE	Good. Instead of that we say, "It was soon after he built the Panama Canal that young Fred Allen — "
ALLEN	Wait a minute, Georgie. Who is going to believe I built the Panama Canal?
GEORGE	Stop worrying, Fred. If there's any trouble and they want proof, we'll call my mother. Go on with your story.
ALLEN	*My* story.

[119]

GEORGE   This book will be bigger than *Uncle Tom's Cabin*. What's next?

ALLEN   Well, after that, I spent three years in Philadelphia.

GEORGE   Three years in Philadelphia . . . In the book that comes out three blank pages.

ALLEN   What's next, Georgie?

GEORGE   Your personal life, Fred. This is the high spot. Who were you in love with? Who were your sweethearts? This is what sells the book, Fred. Take my word for it.

ALLEN   Well, Georgie, I wasn't much of a ladies' man.

GEORGE   This chapter I am calling "True Love and Broken Hearts."

ALLEN   But, Georgie —

GEORGE   On asbestoes I'll write it — "Who lost their hearts to this gallant Casanova? Lillian Russell, Sarah Bernhardt, and the Floradora Sextet."

ALLEN   But you can't say that, Georgie. That's libel.

GEORGE   What libel? On the bottom of the page, in small type, is a footnote — it says: "These people, confidentially, he never met."

ALLEN   Look, Georgie. We're not getting anywhere. Before you make any more notes . . . How much will you charge me to write this book?

GEORGE   For a thousand dollars, I write your Life in ten volumes. And throw in an index.

ALLEN   A thousand dollars. I was planning on something a little cheaper.

[120]

GEORGE   Well. For five hundred dollars I get your life into one book.

ALLEN   Well — I —

GEORGE   Of course, you're not as big a man as you are in ten volumes. But it's a nice fat book. Babies can sit on it, it saves buying a high-chair.

ALLEN   Georgie, what do you write for a hundred dollars?

GEORGE   This is coming out a pamphlet. I write a few dates. You were born . . . You lived; you got on the radio.

ALLEN   That's not so much.

GEORGE   Naturally, for this price you age quickly.

ALLEN   I don't know. A hundred dollars is a lot for a pamphlet. What do I get for fifty?

GEORGE   For fifty dollars it's just a handbill with your picture on it. Underneath I write, "Here is a man with something on the ball."

ALLEN   Just a handbill?

GEORGE   Yes. Just the right size to wrap up your lunch or maybe a herring.

One of our guest stars was responsible for probably the loudest and longest laugh ever heard on radio. The laugh lasted for over forty minutes. Its reverberations may still be echoing among some of the ancient acoustics at NBC. Here is how it happened.

I had read a piece in the *New Yorker* making mention of the arrival in this country of a British lecturer. He sounded

[121]

quite interesting. His name was Captain Knight, and the subject of his lecture was "Falconry." We visited Captain Knight in his hotel quarters and found him chaperoning an ominous-looking eagle named Mr. Ramshaw. Captain Knight agreed to appear on our program bearing eagle.

Accordingly, the Captain appeared on the appointed evening with Mr. Ramshaw riding his wrist sidesaddle. This interview ensued:

ALLEN   What about our guest?

PORTLAND   Our guest tonight is the World's Foremost Authority on Eagles.

ALLEN   An eagle authority, eh? Where did you bump into an eagle expert?

PORTLAND   I heard him on Hobby Lobby last Sunday so I invited him over.

ALLEN   I'd like to see a man whose hobby is eagles.

PORTLAND   Well, here he is. . . . Mr. Allen, meet Captain Charles Knight.

ALLEN   Good evening, Captain Knight.

CAPTAIN   Good evening, Fred.

ALLEN   I — er didn't know that you were bringing an eagle with you tonight, Captain.

CAPTAIN   My eagle won't hurt you, Fred. This is Mr. Ramshaw.

ALLEN   Good er — evening, er — Mr. Ramshaw. He doesn't seem to be warming up to me, Captain Knight.

CAPTAIN   No, Mr. Ramshaw doesn't make friends very

quickly. But he won't hurt you, I give you my word.

ALLEN   Your word. If I can get the eagle's word I'll feel a little more secure. You're sure Mr. Ramshaw likes it there on your wrist?

CAPTAIN   Yes, he's quite contented, Fred. Mr. Ramshaw is a perfect gentleman.

ALLEN   Something tells me you and Mr. Ramshaw are going to end up here at the microphone alone. Possibly with Mr. R. smacking his beak.

CAPTAIN   There's no danger, old boy. Mr. Ramshaw has just eaten.

ALLEN   Fine. Well, first, Captain Knight, your military title and bearing tell me that you have seen service.

CAPTAIN   Yes, Fred. I served in the British Army in the last war.

ALLEN   And after the war you took up the study of bird-life?

CAPTAIN   Not all birds, Fred. I concentrated on the eagle. Today, I am touring the country lecturing and showing films on the eagle. Its life, habits, training and what not.

ALLEN   I imagine, Captain Knight, that the study of the gentleman buzzard is indeed a complex one.

CAPTAIN   Yes. You might say it is rather involved, Fred.

ALLEN   All I know about an eagle is enough to keep away from one. I am a man who hears no eagle, sees no eagle and speaks no eagle. The nearest I have

[123   ]

ever been to an eagle in my life is right now, Captain. And one false move out of Mr. Ramshaw and that was me going through Stamford.

CAPTAIN   You really should make a study of the eagle, Fred.

ALLEN   And there's no time like the present to start, Captain. How many species of this bloated sparrow are there?

CAPTAIN   Well, there are countless varieties of eagle. The most common types in America are the Bald and Golden Eagles.

ALLEN   I see. What is that one we see on the half dollar, a Mint Macaw?

CAPTAIN   No. The fellow on the half dollar is a Bald Eagle.

ALLEN   He is the Jack Benny of the clouds. But what about Mr. Ramshaw here — he isn't a bald eagle wearing a toupee or frown-bib, is he?

CAPTAIN   No, Mr. Ramshaw is a Golden Eagle. Or, to be technical, an *Aquila chrysaetus*.

ALLEN   *Aquila chrysaetus*. Say, I can probably stick John Kieran with that Aquila Chrysaetus and get a spare set of the *Britannica*. Tell me, Captain Knight, is this Golden variety ferocious in its natural state?

CAPTAIN   Oh yes, quite ferocious. I've seen two young Golden Eagles kill each other in a fight, with the mother looking on calmly all the time.

ALLEN   Proving that an eagle's best friend is his father. What do those 10th Avenue canaries eat besides each other?

[124   ]

CAPTAIN   Oh, they live on rabbits, grouse, small lambs —
            almost anything they can carry off safely.

ALLEN   What method do they employ in catching their
            prey?

CAPTAIN   It's all very simple, really. The eagle flies around,
            looking for game. When it spies a victim it swoops
            down suddenly and sinks its talons into it.

ALLEN   And then — blitzkrieg, eh?

CAPTAIN   That is putting it rather mildly, Fred. The eagle's
            talons have a deadly grip.

ALLEN   Yes. I was just looking at those skin stilettos on
            Mr. Ramshaw. I'd like to have his clause in my
            contract. Mr. Ramshaw is looking around, Cap-
            tain, he isn't getting hungrv, by any chance, is
            he?

CAPTAIN   I don't think so, Fred.

ALLEN   Uncle Jim is pigeon-toed. If Mr. Ramshaw is
            nearsighted he might defoot Uncle James.

CAPTAIN   No, the bird is just getting a bit restless, that's all.

ALLEN   I hope it isn't something he's going to eat. He
            certainly is well-behaved for so savage a fowl.
            How were you able to tame him, Captain?

CAPTAIN   Well, fortunately I got him when he was quite
            young. The actual training was a very slow and
            tedious process.

ALLEN   And now that Mr. Ramshaw has attained his ma-
            jority, don't you ever have any trouble handling
            him?

CAPTAIN   Well, occasionally he does get a bit awkward.

He'll take a nip at me, or dig me with his claws.

ALLEN   Is that why you wear that thick glove to protect your hand and arm when Mr. Ramshaw goes to town?

CAPTAIN   Yes, Fred. But when the old boy is on a tantrum, he's apt to nip me right through the glove.

ALLEN   Bites the hand that needs him, eh? How do you quiet Mr. Ramshaw when he's in a temper?

CAPTAIN   I slip a hood over his eyes. Once an eagle is hooded he calms right down.

ALLEN   Yes. It's the same with the Lone Ranger. What does a community-broken eagle eat, Captain?

CAPTAIN   Different meats, as a rule. Mr. Ramshaw's favorites are steak and beef.

ALLEN   Good. I thought you might throw him an acquaintance occasionally. How much does he weigh?

CAPTAIN   Eleven pounds, although he appears much heavier.

ALLEN   He certainly does. He looks like Joe Penner with feathers on. You said, a moment ago, Captain, that you take Ramshaw here around the country with you on all of your lecture tours.

CAPTAIN   Yes, we've traveled from Coast to Coast, Fred.

ALLEN   Don't you have any trouble checking into hotels with him? What happens when you walk up to the desk with the King Kong Robin on your wrist and say, "I'd like to have a double room with a nest?"

CAPTAIN   I never have any trouble, Fred. I only go to hotels where I'm known and they're always glad to welcome Mr. Ramshaw.

ALLEN   But an eagle flying around the lobby —

CAPTAIN   There is no cause for indoor alarm, old boy. Mr. Ramshaw travels in his personal crate.

ALLEN   I see. And where do you quarter him, in your room?

CAPTAIN   Sometimes. At some hotels they let me tie him up near the roof.

ALLEN   What would happen if he ever escaped?

CAPTAIN   He did escape once right here in New York.

ALLEN   Really? How did it happen?

CAPTAIN   Well, Ramshaw and I live at the Hotel Gotham on 55th Street. I generally keep him on the roof there.

ALLEN   Yes.

CAPTAIN   One day I went up to the roof and Ramshaw was gone. I looked out, and there he was, circling about over Radio City.

ALLEN   That's probably how he got talked into going on Hobby Lobby. They book some of their acts beckoning to people from a window. But what did you do with Mr. Ramshaw loose . . . ? Phone American Airlines?

CAPTAIN   No, I informed the police department. In no time every radio car in New York was out looking for him.

ALLEN   Who finally caught him, some fly cop?

CAPTAIN   No, Ramshaw tired and came down that evening. He was found perched on a taxicab going up Madison Avenue.

ALLEN   Probably looking for a taxidermist to give himself up. Well, Captain Knight, it's been nice of you to stop off on your lecture tour and bring Mr. Ramshaw in tonight. Before you go, I wonder if you could have Mr. Ramshaw give us a sample of his flying prowess.

CAPTAIN   Yes. I think perhaps he might enjoy a short flight around the stage here, Fred.

ALLEN   Fine, could he carry my script around with him?

CAPTAIN   Why your script, Fred?

ALLEN   I'll tell you, Captain Knight. It's no novelty for a comedian to see a script get the bird. But when the bird gets a script . . . We'll make radio history, Captain.

CAPTAIN   I see what you mean. But I think Ramshaw would prefer to fly without the script.

ALLEN   He'll ad lib, eh? Well, I'm not telling Ramshaw how to run his business, Captain. It's up to you.

CAPTAIN   Very well. I shall have Mr. Ramshaw fly around the stage and land back on that bandstand. Ready, Ramshaw? Go!

          (Bird flies around stage and lands)

ALLEN   Excellent. A perfect three-claw landing. Right on Van Steeden's bandstand. Any bird will go for the corn in Van Steeden's music. Thanks a lot, Captain.

[128   ]

CAPTAIN   Good night, Fred.

ALLEN   Good night and thank you, Captain Charles Knight.

That was the way it was supposed to end — but Captain Knight and I never did finish this interview. At rehearsal, the eagle's enormous wingspread intrigued me. From the back he looked like Bernarr Macfadden moulting. I thought that the audience might be impressed if Mr. Ramshaw could be persuaded to fly a short distance in the studio and flex his wings for the amazement of those assembled. I apprised Captain Knight of my thought. The Captain somehow conveyed the idea to Mr. Ramshaw. The eagle seemed to understand. In the empty studio, Mr. Ramshaw took off from the Captain's wrist, spread his wings, flew a few feet and grounded himself on top of the bandstand. We tried it several times at rehearsal. Things went smoothly. Mr. Ramshaw even appeared to be enjoying himself.

That night, as the program progressed, everything was fine until Captain Knight read his line, "I shall have Mr. Ramshaw fly around the stage and land back on that bandstand. Ready, Ramshaw? Go!"

And Ramshaw went. He took off from the Captain's wrist gracefully but when he got aloft the glare from the brass instruments in the orchestra (the orchestra had not been at rehearsal) apparently confused him. He couldn't seem to locate the bandstand. He started flying around the studio, his talons clawing the air ad lib. Women were shrieking, afraid that Ramshaw would light on their heads and descalp them. Captain Knight augmented the bedlam by rushing around the studio shouting pertinent instructions in his British accent to the eagle, who was busy wheeling over the audience giving an impression of a buzzard in a moment of indecision. As though he wanted to get as far away from the turmoil as possible, Ramshaw perched on top of a high column up near the ceiling. The imbroglio caused him to forget even the cruder points of etiquette. Mr. Ramshaw gave visual evidence that he was obviously not a housebroken eagle. The visual evidence fortunately just missed the shoulder of a student who had come down from Fordham University to advise me that I had won a popularity poll at the school. He was sitting on the stage after having presented me with a plaque earlier in the show.

As the audience laughed and shouted, the program carried on. Captain Knight was remonstrating with the eagle and advising him to come down from his lofty haven. In one pocket the Captain carried a few chickenheads for emergencies and to sustain Mr. Ramshaw during the day. As he pleaded with the eagle the Captain started to wave a chickenhead as a sort of grisly reward if Ramshaw would abandon his prank and return to captivity. Chaos was in bloom — the Captain with his British hullaballoo, the audience screaming with laughter, the women squealing with fright. Jokes were told, songs were sung, commercials were read. Nothing was heard.

The program went off the air on a note of sustained pandemonium. The Captain despatched a lackey to procure a large raw steak. Apparently Mr. Ramshaw was myopic. From

[130]

his lofty perch he couldn't recognize the tidbit, the chicken-head, in the Captain's waving hand. The king-sized steak, however, he did identify. Mr. Ramshaw flew back to the Captain's wrist and his supper.

After the excitement had become passé noise, I received a note from an NBC executive taking me to task for instigating this huggermugger. The executive received this reply:

Dear Sir:

Am in receipt of your communiqué commenting on *l'affaire eagle,* as they are calling it around the advertising agency.

I thought I had seen about everything in radio but the eagle had a trick up his feathered colon that was new to me.

An acolyte from your quarters brought news to us, following the nine o'clock broadcast, that the eagle was to be grounded at the midnight show. It was quite obvious that Mr. Ramshaw, as the eagle is known around the Falcon Lounge at the Audubon Society Rooms, resented your dictatorial orders. When his cue came to fly, and he was still bound to Captain Knight's wrist, Mr. Ramshaw, deprived by nature of the organs essential in the voicing of an audible complaint, called upon other anatomical regions to wreak upon us his rebuttal to your martinet ban.

Toscanini, your house man, has foisted some movements on studio audiences in 8–H, the Bulova Company has praised its movement over your network facilities, but when Radio City is being torn down, to make way for another parking lot, the one movement that will be recalled will be the eagle's movement on Wednesday last.

If you have never seen a ghost's beret you could have viewed one on Mr. Rockefeller's carpet during our sterling performance.

I know you await with trepidation the announcement that I am going to interview Sabu with his elephant some week.

Yours for a wet broom in 8–H on Wednesday nights.

FRED ALLEN

Every October, when we returned to open the radio season, we tried to have one new feature in the program. One year we presented the college competitions. The idea was to interest college boys and girls in our show and to tap a source of talent new to radio. We corresponded with colleges all over the country until thirty-nine of them had agreed to cooperate. We sent an advance man ahead to arrange the first student auditions. Some days later, a second representative attended the final audition. We did not participate in any way except to pay the bills. The students ran their own auditions and selected their final winner. The prize was a trip to New York with all expenses paid and $100 in cash.

The college talent was very successful. The winners received considerable publicity in the local papers and somehow the name of our program always showed up in the story. We uncovered some excellent talent. There was one problem, however. Some weeks there was a bit of logrolling at the college and the winner who showed up to appear on the program was not the most talented but the most popular student on the campus. On more than one occasion a beautiful girl arrived with plenty of curves and a flat voice. The trumpets and violins had to function fortissimo to subdue her rendition. One college sent as its most talented student a lightning calculator. A mathematical wizard didn't make much sense in radio. We had to give the calculator the first prize and substitute a girl singer who had come in second in the final audition.

As the weeks went by, the students tried to outdo each other in presenting me with weird presents. At the end of the season I could have opened a thrift shop. I had a set of false teeth, a bucket of coal, an eighteen-foot oar filched from a scull, a fire hat, a pair of Indian moccasins, a cellophane Stetson hat and other high-class trash. From Tuskegee Institute, the late George Washington Carver sent me a hundred-pound bag of peanuts. When the burlap bag was delivered to the studio the actors had slit its side. By the time I had an opportunity to examine my gift about forty pounds of peanuts had departed the premises accompanied. When the goober snatchers arrived home they found that Dr. Carver had sent me raw peanuts.

The University of Chicago Round Table was the first informal discussion group to attain success in radio. The members of the Round Table were three University of Chicago professors. For thirty minutes they talked extemporaneously, exploring the facets of a vital issue currently in the news. The subject was changed each week and so were the professors. The listeners, I assume, were the same.

With the Round Table riding the crest the depths were not being ignored. Our program suddenly acquired a new feature called the Average Man's Round Table. At its première we explained to the audience that the only people you heard giving their opinions over the radio were the big people. The little people, the nobodies of the nation, had no forum from which they could air their views. We allotted the Average Man's Round Table ten minutes of our radio time to make it possible for unimportant citizens to discuss the issues that were influencing their lives.

As we planned them, the ten-minute sessions were to be unrehearsed. This posed a major censorship problem. The network and the sponsor both felt that selecting people from the studio audience, permitting them to analyze the political situation and comment on people in the news, might result in legal complications.

We were advised to restrict our discussion topics to harmless subjects. We did. For two seasons the average man had an opportunity to appear on our program and grapple with such minor questions as:

"Do you think tipping should be abolished?"

"Should motorists, in addition to passing eye tests, physical tests and driving tests, be required to pass an intelligence test?"

"When problems confront a child, to which parent should the child turn? Does Mother know best? Or does Father know better?"

"In what form do you most enjoy a story? Do you prefer to read it, see it as a stage play, or hear it over the radio?"

This gives you an idea of the competition we were giving the University of Chicago Round Table.

The coming of radio, and his access to the microphone,

resulted in the average man's discovery of his ego. In vaudeville, years before, a magician had his troubles coaxing a
member of the audience up on the stage to witness the
magician "sawing a woman in halves" or "impaling a small
Hindu concealed in a wicker basket on the point of a blunt
sword." The magician spent many minutes pleading, and
assuring that nobody would be ridiculed during his performance, before one lone person would overpower his
modesty, mount the stage and stand terrified before the
audience.

Today, the Man in the Street does his broadcast hiding in
a doorway. He is afraid to show himself in public. The minute
his microphone is sighted a motley throng is on him. Soiled
matrons eager to divulge how they first met their husbands.
Tottering old men outfrailing each other to get to the mike
and explain how they became ancient. Gamy adolescents
vying to flaunt their arrogance.

Are we making progress? The University of Chicago Round
Table has gone! The morons are still here!

When the Texas Company started to sponsor the program
they didn't want to have it appear that they had merely taken
over the old Ipana and Sal Hepatica show. The announcer,
who was identified with the drug company's products, had to
be replaced, a new orchestra, Al Goodman's, was acquired, a
new singer was added. The cast, however, remained un-
changed. The Texaco Workshop Players were actually the
Mighty Allen Art Players incognito.

For the new sponsor we started on a new network — leaving

NBC to go to CBS. The new network's pet project was the Columbia Workshop, a talented group of young writers and directors doing experimental work in the new medium.

In a short time the Columbia Workshop had competition. The Texaco Workshop Players were doing experimental work of this nature — one of the first specimens to escape from our test tube was the episode involving Orson Welles.

PORTLAND   Who is your guest?

ALLEN   That's my trouble. I had a telegram from Orson Welles saying he wants to see me tonight.

PORTLAND   Orson Welles!

ALLEN   That's the way I feel about it, too. What he wants to see me —
                (Knock at door)

PORTLAND   That's Orson Welles! *(Shrieks)*

ALLEN   Portland, control yourself! Come in!
                (Door opens)

ALLEN   Yes?

TECHNICIAN   Is this the microphone Mr. Welles is going to use.

ALLEN   Yes, this —

TECHNICIAN   Step aside, Buddy. One! Two! Three! Woof! Woof! Hello, Max! One, Two, Three, Woof, Woof. Hello, Max!

ALLEN   Just a minute, friend. What is this?

TECHNICIAN   I'm Mr. Welles's personal chief technician.

ALLEN   And you check ——

TECHNICIAN   Right. This microphone may be all right for a schnook like you, but for Mr. Welles it's gotta be perfect. One, Two, Three, Woof, Woof. Hello, Max. One, Two —

(Phone rings)

TECHNICIAN That phone's for me. It's Max; Max is my superior.

ALLEN Anybody would be your superior.

TECHNICIAN Hello, Max? Right, Max. I should report to Mr. Welles it's okay. Okay, Max.

ALLEN All right. If you're through —

TECHNICIAN Wait a minute. What's these scratches on the microphone?

ALLEN Our announcer, Mr. Godfrey, has buck teeth.

TECHNICIAN I hope Mr. Welles don't notice it.

ALLEN Do you think I should spray the microphone with perfume?

TECHNICIAN With you around it wouldn't hurt none, brother.

(Door slams)

ALLEN Orson Welles. Special technicians he has to have, to go on the air. All the President needs is two logs and a Boy Scout.

PORTLAND I'm getting scared.

ALLEN Why?

PORTLAND Maybe Mr. Welles is coming here to get even with you.

ALLEN Even for what? I had nothing to do with *Citizen Kane*.

PORTLAND I know. But you told all those jokes about Orson Welles.

[137]

ALLEN	That was last year. What can he do —
	(Knock at door)
PORTLAND	Orson Welles! *(Shrieks)*
ALLEN	Portland! Quiet! Come in!
	(Door opens)
SISSY	Excuse me. I shan't be a minute. *(Calls)* Hello, out there! *(Louder)* HELLO, OUT THERE! *(Louder)* HELLO, OUT THERE!
ALLEN	Look, brother . . .
SISSY	Quiet, please. *(Coyly)* Hello, out there!
ALLEN	What is this?
SISSY	I am Mr. Welles's personal acoustical diagnostician.
ALLEN	Oh.
SISSY	I'm testing the acoustics.
ALLEN	I see.
SISSY	If Mr. Welles doesn't like the acoustics you may have to tear down part of the studio. *Ta-ta!*
ALLEN	We should wreck the building. Stop trembling, Portland.
PORTLAND	But I'm scared.
ALLEN	Don't be silly. If Mr. Welles is coming up here about those jokes I told about him last year, why should I worry? I've never seen a genius with muscles yet. If he wants to start . . .
	(Knock at door. Door opens fast)
ALLEN	Now what?
DOCTOR	*(Sniffs three or four times)*

[138]

ALLEN   What's with this sniffing, Mister? Who are you?

DOCTOR   I'm Mr. Welles's personal physician. *(Sniff . . .*
Sniff)

ALLEN   But what —

DOCTOR   I'm checking the air in here to see if it's fit for
Mr. Welles to breathe. *(Sniff . . . Sniff)*

ALLEN   Everybody else is breathing this air.

DOCTOR   Mr. Welles is a great artist; he's a very sensitive
man.

ALLEN   Sensitive . . . He was on Benny's Program last
spring. If he can stand that he can stand anything.

DOCTOR   Mr. Welles had a cold that night. Good-by!
(Door slams)

PORTLAND   Mr. Welles sure doesn't take any chances, does
he?

ALLEN   I wish I knew what he wanted to see me about.
I'm getting nervous myself now.
(Knock on door . . . fast. Door opens)

ALL   *(Hum of voices)*

ALLEN   Hey, wait a minute, you guys.

STAGE HAND   *(Fast)* Beat it, Bud. Slim! You and Mike roll
that red plush carpet from Mr. Welles's car
right to the microphone.

MIKE   Okay.

STAGE HAND   Sam! Have you got your trumpet ready for the
fanfare?

SAM   Standin' by, sir.

ALLEN   Look, fellers.

STAGE HAND	Will you get out of the way. Slim! Light the incense and get the spotlights ready.
SLIM	Okay.
SAM	Mr. Welles is stepping out of his car.
STAGE HAND	For Pete's sake! Hurry with that rug.
ALLEN	Here, let me help.
SAM	Mr. Welles is entering the building!
STAGE HAND	Hit those spotlights!
ALLEN	Get that rug down.
SAM	Mr. Welles is here.
STAGE HAND	The fanfare, Sam! Presenting —
	(Fanfare by orchestra)
ALL	Mr. Orson Welles!
	(Applause)
ALLEN	Well, good evening, Mr. Welles.
ORSON	Excuse me. *(Tests mike)* One, two, three! Woof! Woof! Hello Max!
ALLEN	The microphone has been tested, Mr. Welles.
ORSON	Good. *(Calls)* Hello, out there! Hello, out there!
ALLEN	The acoustics have been checked, Mr. Welles.
ORSON	Good. *(Sniffs three or four times)*
ALLEN	The air has been approved.
ORSON	Very good. I'm a busy man.
ALLEN	I know.
ORSON	I am very happy to be here on the Phillip Morris Program this evening.
ALLEN	That was Friday night.
ORSON	Oh, yes. What night is this?

[140   ]

ALLEN   Sunday. This is the Texaco Star Theater. My name is Allen.

ORSON   Fred Allen?

ALLEN   Yes.

ORSON   How do you do, Mr. Allen.

ALLEN   Mr. Welles, I'm thrilled. —

ORSON   Naturally. I'll come to the point, Mr. Allen. Last year, on your program you said several derogatory things about me.

ALLEN   Oh, I say, you haven't met Portland yet, Mr. Welles. She's dying to meet you. Portland!

PORTLAND   Yes.

ALLEN   Portland, this is Orson Welles.

ORSON   Hello, Portland.

PORTLAND   *(Screams. Runs away)*

ORSON   What's the matter with that child? Was that a shriek?

ALLEN   No. She has asthma — it's pitched high.

ORSON   Well, let's get down to business, Mr. Allen. About those derogatory remarks . . .

ALLEN   I don't recall —

ORSON   Do you remember what you said about my home in Hollywood?

ALLEN   No. I don't —

ORSON   Perhaps I can refresh your memory. You were talking about those trick doorbells they have out in Hollywood.

ALLEN   Oh, those fancy chime effects.

ORSON   Yes. You said when a person rang my doorbell,

[141]

sixteen peacocks flew out of the transom, a man in a belfry in the hall pealed his bell, twenty-one guns went off in a salute, and I came out of four doors simultaneously.

ALLEN   I must have been stuck for a joke that night. I don't remember.

ORSON   And that time you were discussing Hollywood Victory Gardens. What was it you said?

ALLEN   I just said that all you did was go out to your back yard, point to the ground and say "Grow!" and fourteen acres of corn sprang up. I'm sorry if you —

ORSON   Well, that was last year. I'm here to speak to you about this year.

ALLEN   Mr. Welles. Believe me. I haven't made a single crack about you this year. I wasn't even planning to. I swear it.

ORSON   What's the matter, Fred? Don't you like me any more?

ALLEN   You're not mad, Orson?

ORSON   Not at all, Fred. I enjoy a good laugh as well as anybody.

ALLEN   Well, Orson, this is a great surprise to me.

ORSON   Why, Fred?

ALLEN   I always pictured you as a man from another planet, a transcendentalist, a genius, a legend in the making — and here you are, joking and laughing with little old egg-laying me.

ORSON   Fred, I wish somebody would do something

about this Superman myth the public has swallowed about me. It's embarrassing. After all, I'm just an ordinary guy.

ALLEN   I know, Orson. But your early life has been shrouded in mystery. If people were told something about your childhood they would know you are not a cross between Flash Gordon and a Quiz Kid. You're just another man in the street.

ORSON   What's there to tell, Fred? I was born in Chicago. Like any other kid I went through grammar school and at the age of five I entered Northwestern University.

ALLEN   At five you entered college?

ORSON   As a sophomore. I skipped the freshman year. My college days were uneventful. I majored in Esperanto. . . .

ALLEN   I see.

ORSON   Well, I got out of college at seven, *magna cum laude*. I hung around with Einstein awhile. We tiffed one day over a bit of calculus. I rejected Einstein's theory. At the age of twelve I resigned from the Smithsonian Institute and went into the theater.

ALLEN   And the rest is history.

ORSON   It's been nothing, Fred. So I've had a little success in the theater, radio and pictures. Does that mean I'm a genius? I wear the same clothes as other men, I eat the same food. And like any

[143]

ordinary guy who works hard, my feet hurt at the end of the day.

ALLEN   No wonder. Trying to squeeze fourteen toes in an ordinary pair of shoes. But, tell me, are you back from Hollywood for good?

ORSON   No, I'm just giving Hollywood a short breathing spell.

ALLEN   Are you going to do a play in New York?

ORSON   I don't think so, Fred. Broadway seems to be stressing burlesque this season and I can't see myself doing a strip-tease.

ALLEN   You can't tell. Gypsy Rose Welles. Or a Shakespearean revival, All's Welles That Ends Welles.

ORSON   No, Fred. I'm going back into radio for the Lockheed company. That's really why I wanted to talk to you tonight.

ALLEN   About your new program?

ORSON   Yes.

ALLEN   If I can give you some hints, or introduce you to Ma Perkins, I'd be —

ORSON   No, Fred. I'm getting along in years. I have finally come to the conclusion that I can no longer carry on alone. I need a co-star. An actor with a flair for the buskin. A man with dramatic distingué. An artist who can match my dramatic ability.

ALLEN   You have found such an actor, Orson?

ORSON   Yes, Fred. You!

[144]

ALLEN   Me? Orson, Gad, this is an honor. What is your first play?

ORSON   We'll do Victor Hugo's great story, *Les Misérables*. You will co-star with me.

ALLEN   Just you and I do the entire play?

ORSON   It will be fifty-fifty. I'll play Jean Valjean.

ALLEN   And I?

ORSON   You will play the French detective, Javert.

ALLEN   Javert, eh? *Je suis ze law.*

ORSON   Oh. Do you speak French, Fred?

ALLEN   Just enough to get out of Rumpelmayers, Orson.

ORSON   That will help a lot. If we can rehearse a minute we'll run over the play here before I go.

ALLEN   Okay. We'll present our co-starring epic, *Les Misérables*, immediately following a short selection by Mr. Goodman. . . . Allen and Welles. Gosh! . . .

ALLEN   And now, Ladies and Gentlemen, Mr. Welles and I present our dramatic highlight of the evening. Are you ready, Orson?

ORSON   Yes, Fred. You have your part?

ALLEN   Yes. Frankly, I'm a little nervous.

ORSON   You'll be all right, Fred. You're with me in every scene.

ALLEN   We're co-stars.

ORSON   Yes. Everything is fifty-fifty.

ALLEN   How does the play start?

[145]

ORSON	I'll do the narration, Fred. I have to set the scene. Can I have some appropriate music?
ALLEN	You bet! Mr. Goodman, appropriate music for Mr. Welles, please.
ORCHESTRA	*(Heavy dramatic music . . . Fades)*
ORSON	*(Dramatic) Les Misérables!* Victor Hugo's immortal story of a soul transfigured and redeemed, through suffering. This is an Orson Welles production.
REED	Radio version of *Les Misérables* prepared by —
ORSON	Orson Welles!
REED	Directed by —
ORSON	Orson Welles!
REED	Starring —
ORSON	Orson Welles! During Orson Welles's presentation of *Les Misérables,* Mr. Welles will be assisted by that sterling dramatic actor of stage, screen and radio, Mr. —
ORCHESTRA	*(Heavy dramatic music . . . Fades quickly)*
ALLEN	Hold it! Hold it! Wait a minute, Orson.
ORSON	Is something wrong, Fred?
ALLEN	All I've heard so far is Orson Welles. If I'm costarring at least my name should be mentioned.
ORSON	I announced you, Fred. The music cut in too quickly.
ALLEN	Watch that, Mr. Goodman. I have a public, too, you know. Mr. Welles, I'm no bit player. You may have your Mercury Theater, but don't for-

get, I've been a star with the Mighty Allen Art
Players for a decade.

ORSON   I wish you wouldn't be so impulsive, Fred. *Les
Misérables* is the story of two men, Jean Valjean,
the hunted convict, liberated after serving nine-
teen long years in the galleys — and Javert, the
merciless minion of the law. You're on Jean Valjean's trail all through the play.

ALLEN   I'm Javert and you are Jean Valjean.

ORSON   That's right. Each character is equally important
to the story. It's fifty-fifty.

ALLEN   Okay. Let's go.

ORSON   The first scene is a dingy garret in the slums of
Paris. As the story opens I am hiding out. I
think I have escaped you. As we first see Jean
Valjean he is soliloquizing.

ORCHESTRA   *(Heavy dramatic music . . . Fades)*

ORSON   *(Dramatic)* At last, Jean Valjean, you are safe.
There is no cause to fear. This Javert who has
hounded you so long. His fearful instinct which
seemed to have divined the truth, that had divined it. And which followed me everywhere.
That merciless bloodhound always in pursuit of
me, is finally thrown off the track, absolutely
baffled. *(Dramatic laugh)* But hark! That sound
upon the stairs! Footsteps! Those same plodding
footsteps!

         (Knock at door)

ORSON   Javert! What is to be done? Ah, this window!

Jean Valjean will never be taken! Good-by, Javert!

(Knock at door)

ORCHESTRA   *(Heavy dramatic music . . . Fades)*

ALLEN   Hey, wait a minute, Orson.

ORSON   Later, Fred. We start the second scene now.

ALLEN   Well, never mind the second scene. What about that first scene?

ORSON   Why, it was fifty-fifty.

ALLEN   But you took both fifties.

ORSON   That's ridiculous, Fred. You stole the whole scene.

ALLEN   I did?

ORSON   What broke up Jean Valjean's soliloquy? What caused him to leap through that open window?

ALLEN   I —

ORSON   It was that knock on the door. And who knocked on that door? Javert.

ALLEN   Javert. I play Javert.

ORSON   You motivate the entire story. If you hadn't knocked at the door I'd still be in that garret. We'd have no play.

ALLEN   Oh.

ORSON   In this second scene you steal the whole thing. I'm just a foil.

ALLEN   A foil. That sounds good. What is the second scene?

ORSON   It's years later. This time, you, Javert, have me trapped. Cosette Fabantou, a demimonde, is

[148]

concealing me in the back room of a bistro. I, Jean Valjean, am pacing up and down.

ORCHESTRA   *(Heavy dramatic music . . . Fades)*

COSETTE   *(French)* Jean! Will you stop pacing? *Toujours* up and down.

ORSON   This is the end, Cosette, my farewell to freedom. Instead of liberty waits the galley crew, the iron collar, the chain at my foot — fatigue, the dungeon, the plank-bed — all of the horrors I know so well. To be tumbled about by the jailer's stick. To have my bare feet in iron-bound shoes. To submit morning and evening to the hammer of the roundsman who tests the fetters. Time is short, the net is tightening.

      (Police whistle)

ORSON   Javert!

COSETTE   Quick, Jean Valjean, through this trapdoor.

ORSON   Merci, Cosette! Jean Valjean will never be taken again. *A'voir*, Javert!

      (Police whistle)

ORCHESTRA   *(Heavy music . . . Fast fade)*

ALLEN   Hold it! Hold it! Now, look, Orson —

ORSON   Fred, you were magnificent.

ALLEN   I was —

ORSON   You stole that scene right out from under my nose.

ALLEN   I stole the scene again?

ORSON   Gad, that suspense, man.

ALLEN   Suspense? Aw — I —

[149]

ORSON   I've seen Javert played a hundred times. The Theatre Guild, The Grand Guignol, Eddie Dowling, have played Javert. But I've never heard a Javert get the tone out of that police whistle that you got tonight.

ALLEN   Look, Orson, I don't want to hog the thing. But in two acts all I've done is knock on a door and blow a whistle. After all, I'm an actor, not a soundman. When do I get to read some lines?

ORSON   The next scene is all yours, Fred. Your speech is the climax of the entire play.

ALLEN   Now, we're getting some place. What's next?

ORSON   In this final scene you trail me through the sewers of Paris. You finally corner me single-handed, there we stand, face to face — I have just a few words and then you speak.

ALLEN   I speak. Good. Let's go!

ORCHESTRA   *(Heavy music . . . Fades)*

ORSON   *(Dramatic)* Mon Doo! Alone in this sewer! Trapped like a rat who nightly crawls through this hideous muck of the city. The gloomy darkness, this narrow archway above my head, these two slimy corridor walls. Sluice as far as the eye can see. Filth and offal dance on this sea of scum. But hark! That sloshing through the muck. Javert! At last you've cornered me, Javert! Don't talk, Javert! Before you seal my doom, I would speak for the last time. You will never take Jean Valjean alive, Javert. *(Laughs)* The

[150   ]

water in this sewer is rising, Javert. I am six
feet nine. You, Javert, are five feet two. The
water rises, Javert. There is no turning back.
The water — higher — higher . . . Now, Javert,
you have Jean Valjean at your mercy. Pronounce
my doom. Speak, Javert. Speak.

ALLEN   *(Gargles water and tries to talk)*

ORCHESTRA *(Music up to finish)*

Falstaff Openshaw, the Bowery Bard, was the first comedy
character to make a weekly appearance on our show. Every
week, for many years, we had been inventing a variety of
grotesque characters that could be impersonated by our cast
of actors. Listeners tired of stooges they heard week after
week. When a comedy character was new his dialect or his
catchline started people laughing the minute the stooge
opened his mouth. There was a sort of lazy psychology involved in this reaction. The listener knew everything the
stooge was going to say. He anticipated every line. He didn't
have to think. He could laugh from memory. When we started
writing our show I felt that if we could conjure up good
comedy material and have it performed by versatile actors,
who were kept anonymous, our comedy group's artistic life
would be far longer than the normal span of the popular
weekly stooge.

Many people wondered how Falstaff Openshaw happened
to step out of limbo to raucous up the kilocycles with his
poems and bombast. Some weeks when we were writing the

[151]

Town Hall News, items were scarce. To fill out the time we would use but one news subject broken up into interviews and ending with a short sketch. If we had difficulty sustaining the idea, occasionally I would produce an itinerant poet, named Thorndyke Swinburne, to recite something he had written for the occasion. The device usually worked well and when we finally decided to permanently confine the news to one subject and a series of interviews, the poet character seemed to be ideal to bring the episode to a hilarious close.

The synthetic name, Falstaff Openshaw, came from two sources. Falstaff from Sir John Falstaff, a character in Shakespeare's Henry IV. Openshaw was borrowed from a man who was working in a shipyard up in Maine. Shakespeare couldn't sue us. Mr. Openshaw didn't. It was a happy arrangement.

Falstaff Openshaw was successful from the start. To preface his weekly masterpiece Falstaff would list some of the newer works he had been working on in his dactyl lab.

You may remember:

> *Come with me to the belfry, Nellie*
> *We'll kick the gong around.*

> *Back the patrol to the sidewalk, Sergeant*
> *That step's too high for my mother.*

Falstaff's weekly visit started in this vein:

FALSTAFF   Tarry, Lumpkin, don't skidaddle, Falstaff's here with Fiddle-Faddle.

[152]

ALLEN   Falstaff Openshaw!

FALSTAFF   The rancid Rabelais is yours to command.

ALLEN   You haven't warmed over another set of those rhymed monstrosities?

FALSTAFF   Have you heard:
             Said the Big Bull Moose, Oh, What's the Use?
             As he snorted adieu to the little Goose . . . ?

ALLEN   No.

FALSTAFF   *She was only the Ashman's Daughter, that's why she was down in the Dumps . . . ?*

ALLEN   No.

FALSTAFF   *There's no meter on the patrol, Mother, you don't have to pay for your ride . . . ?*

ALLEN   Now wait a minute, Falstaff. That is enough out of you. Tonight we are talking about colleges and graduation.

FALSTAFF   Precisely why I am here. I have written a poem.

ALLEN   What is your college poem called?

FALSTAFF   "To College I Say Poo!"

ALLEN   How does it go?

FALSTAFF   *I hear old grads rave about*
                 The college days they knew,
                 Their alma mater and their class —
                 But to college I say — Poo!

                 I went to college four long years,
                 I studied Latin and Greek,
                 Spanish, Eskimo, Swedish and French —
                 Eight foreign tongues I speak.

I mastered the classics, physics and law,
Economics and Invertebrate Zoology.
Advanced Qualitative Organic Analysis
I passed along with Psychology.

I got an A.B., Ph.D., and B.S.
I translated the entire Koran,
I was Valedictorian of my class
And today — I'm a Good Humor man!

On June 28, 1942, from midnight to 1 A.M. we did our final full-hour program. Ours was the last of the comedy hour shows in radio. Times had changed. Costs had increased and the salaries of the stars, who could attract audiences, had risen so high that an executive mentioning an actor's salary was risking a nosebleed in conference. Many of the half-hour shows had been reduced to fifteen minutes. The hour shows had either completely disappeared or been halved to thirty minutes. When the Texas Company decided to do a half-hour program the next October it took a load off my mind. I knew how a baldheaded man felt after removing his toupee on a hot day.

For eight years, 39 weeks each year, we had written and performed a 60-minute program. The first show was done in New York, from 9 to 10 P.M., for the Eastern audience. Three hours later we did a repeat show. (The use of transcriptions was unknown at that time.) A repeat show meant just that. Our cast had to return to the studio at midnight and repeat the entire program for the audience in California and the West Coast.

The work involved in writing and assembling a weekly radio show began to seem like a recipe for a nervous breakdown. During the early years it was fun. At this point it was drudgery. I was reading nine newspapers a day looking for subject matter for jokes, topical ideas we could use for news vignettes, unusual characters we could interview on People You Didn't Expect to Meet, motion picture and play reviews to check pictures and stage shows we could burlesque and whose stars we might book as guests. Walking along the street, riding in cabs or in the subway, I always had my head in a newspaper or magazine. Every few minutes I was tearing some item out of something and stuffing it into a pocket. As the day wore on my pockets seemed to be herringbone goiters and I looked as though I was a walking wastebasket.

Our weekly schedule was a treadmill made up of seven revolving days. Our second broadcast was finished at 1 A.M. on Thursday. The minute the show was over, the two writers, the director and I quit the studio and adjourned to a runt-sized delicatessen which was deserted at that hour. After ordering our food we started to hash over the next week's show and the problems it presented. The program had four separate parts to accommodate four commercials. Every week, we needed a news-reel segment, a routine for Portland leading into People You Didn't Expect to Meet, a guest-star idea and comedy dialogue and a final sketch for the cast. As we ate the writers explained a synopsis they had worked out for the next sketch. Between bites and slurps of coffee we exchanged ideas. When we had agreed on the progression of the sketch plot, the individual scenes to be used and the comedy finish, the writers put their notes away. Next, we would discuss the People You Didn't Expect to Meet routine. One of the writers was to interview the person the following day. If we had a gentleman who stuffed sausage we would try to think of the things a person listening at home might like to know about the art of bologna taxidermy. Questions were written down and when we had exhausted the subject, or the writer felt that he had sufficient material to enable him to cross-examine the sausage stuffer thoroughly, desserts were ordered and we took up the next item on our nocturnal agenda. This usually involved the guest star. If we had a Hollywood celebrity we decided what subject matter might be used for comedy purposes, recent films, future plans if any, etc. This was one of my departments. I made notes and discussed jokes and current Hollywood gossip so that I would be fortified when I found myself in the presence of the film celebrity the next afternoon. It was 3 or 3:30 A.M. before we quit the delicatessen with the cold cuts and the assorted program material under control.

Thursday, I slept late. Arriving home at 4 A.M. I would try to sleep. Most of my body would make contact with Morpheus but my stomach always seemed to stay wide awake. I have always felt that the stomach is a selfish organ. When you eat late and then go to bed the stomach can't rest because it has all of that digesting to do. The rest of the body goes to sleep leaving the stomach to cope with its chores. The stomach gets lonesome. That is why you can't close your eyes after a late meal, your stomach likes to feel that it isn't up alone at that hour. Thursday afternoon I would visit the guest star, explain what we planned to do on the program, invite suggestions, make my notes and return home. Thursday night I wrote no matter how late until I had finished the first draft of the guest spot.

Friday, I worked on fan mail all day. The growing popularity of the program brought an increased number of requests. Friends, strangers and organizations needing money. Benefit committees eternally requesting an appearance for some worthy cause. Photographs to be mailed out to hundreds of children who had sent in the scrubby information that their hobby was collecting photos of radio favorites and lucky you — you were their favorite. Much of the routine mail was handled by a secretary but there were always enough problems in the mail to kill an entire day and me along with it. Friday night, Portland and I had our night out. A theater, a movie, or to visit friends.

Saturday, all of the newspaper clips I had torn out of the various newspapers and magazines during the week were sorted and examined. A subject was selected for the news reel. Other highlights in the news were set aside to be used in an opening monologue or in Portland's routine. Saturday afternoon, the writers brought the People You Didn't Expect to Meet interview and the sketch we had worked on in the delicatessen. Saturday night I rewrote, cut down and worked on the writers' two scripts.

Sunday was a long day. After church, I would spend the day writing the news reels, a poem for Falstaff, the opening monologue, Portland's routine, the announcements leading into the commercials — and assemble and blend the entire show content before I went to bed. When the secretary finished at 4 or 5 A.M. the script was left with the night man at the apartment house to be picked up by a Western Union boy at 8 A.M. to have copies mimeographed and ready for rehearsal on Monday.

Monday, late in the morning I got up somehow and went to the barbershop. The barber would pelt me around the head with cold towels to help me come to life such as it was. At 1 P.M. the cast gathered at the studio for the first reading of the script. After two readings over the microphones we knew what was going to play funny and what we would have to abandon or rewrite. The writers, the director and I made notes during the readings. The show was timed. The cast was dismissed. Sandwiches and milk shakes or coffee were served and consumed while each person checked the notes and suggestions he had made during the rehearsal. Every line of dialogue was combed to see if it could be tightened or improved. During the three hour session the best suggestions were adopted and the changes made. After this ordeal Portland and I would have dinner and then I went home to go over some fifty pages of dialogue alone. I worked through the night again to make a final version of the program to be done on the air.

Tuesday, when the final script was mimeographed, one copy went to the NBC Continuity Acceptance Department for legal and censorship checks. One copy went to the sponsor's office. Another copy went to the advertising agency. These were the three sources at which the comedian's troubles originated. We had to be available on Tuesday, ready to make any script changes or defend any joke in the script that had aroused anyone of sufficient importance to compel us to react to his comment. Tuesday afternoon, the writers, the director and I met to discuss a plot for the sketch the following week. This enabled the writers to give it some thought before we met late the next night.

Wednesday, the day of the program, rehearsal started at 10 A.M. The dialogue, musical numbers and commercials were rehearsed in different studios. At 1 P.M. the dress rehearsal was held. This was the first time the entire show had been assembled. Usually the hour script would be eight or ten minutes too long. From 2 to 6.30 P.M., after hearing the comment of the gardenia-bearing gentlemen from the sponsor's and advertising agency's offices, the show was trimmed to fit an exact hour. During the sixty minutes seven minutes were allowed for laughter and applause. At 9 P.M. the show, cut down to fifty-three minutes, went on the air. At midnight, the repeat show went on what was left of the air. At 1 A.M., the minute the show was over, the two writers, the director and I quit the studio and adjourned to the runt-sized delicatessen to get back on our treadmill.

After eight years of this weekly hour-show routine, when the Texas Company wanted to do a half-hour program I was as happy dividing as a rabbit is multiplying . . . if I may permit myself a colloquialism.

PART IV

Allen's Alley

There is an old Lithuanian fable that has never been translated as far as I know. It tells about the two Siamese twins who were going through life looking as though they had just stepped out of Noah's ark. One twin was always complaining. Every morning he'd say to himself, "Look at the trouble I have dressing. I have to put on two union suits, two suits of clothes, two pairs of shoes and shave two faces. If I could only disperse myself I'd be two separate people and I personally would only have to do half of this work." One summer, the twins went to the Siamese convention. Their hotel reservations couldn't be found. The two boys had to take a small room with twin beds. That night, after the Siamese twins had listened to their favorite radio show, Double or Nothing, when they tried to get into the twin beds they realized that they were stretching the thing too far. They started to fight among themselves. The police were called. The Siamese twins tried to escape through the window. The complaining twin was caught. The other one got away. Now that he was finally alone the Siamese twin was still complaining. Every morning he'd say to himself, "Look at the trouble I have dressing. I have two union suits and only one body, four shoes and only two feet, two razors and only one face. I always have something left over." The moral is: If the grass is always greener in the other fellow's yard — let him worry about cutting it.

I had never heard this old Lithuanian fable but I sure was in the same predicament as the complaining Siamese twin. Condensing the hour show to the half hour "I always had something left over." Instead of the four comedy spots, in the shorter show, we could only do two. The relaxed type of dialogue of the longer routines had to be replaced by brisk, staccato lines. For the first few programs I felt like a man who for years had been writing on the *Encyclopaedia Britannica* and suddenly started to write for *Reader's Digest*.

It took some time to get accustomed to the new format. Instead of the long interviews with odd characters and the people in the news we now had a first section called Allen's Alley. In the ten minutes we formerly consumed masticating the gristle with nonentities at the Round Table sessions we now presented guest stars in an original comedy sketch or a plot that enabled them to do their vocal or instrumental specialties.

When we were trying to decide what we could salvage from the old program, the first asset that came to mind was Portland. My artistic life was hectic and I didn't want to have any trouble at home. Portland is a fine cook and I knew that if the new show changed her status for the worse my goose would be cooked and she knew how to cook it.

Portland's role actually became more important. Using but one news event for Allen's Alley, Portland took over some of the functions of the old news reel. I was able to tell many additional topical jokes that couldn't otherwise have been used.

Portland's new routine ran the gamut. To wit:

PORTLAND   Mr. Allen, Mama said you were born in Boston.

ALLEN   That's true, Portland. In those days there was no bird life in Boston. The stork brought me as far as Providence, and the American Express Company delivered me the rest of the way.

PORTLAND   Does every boy born in Boston *have* to go to Harvard?

ALLEN   It isn't compulsory. If you know the right people you can get out of it.

PORTLAND   I knew a boy whose uncle died and left him a pair of dirty sport shoes and a crew haircut.

ALLEN   And?

PORTLAND   He *had* to go to Harvard.

ALLEN   With dirty sport shoes and a crew haircut he didn't have a chance. I knew a boy whose uncle died and left him a short raincoat. He had to go to Princeton.

PORTLAND   That story about you in the magazine said you worked in the Boston Public Library.

ALLEN   Yes, I was a finger-wetter. When women wearing veils were reading and wanted to turn a page they couldn't wet their fingers unless they raised their veils. The women would signal. I would rush over, wet their fingers, and withdraw.

PORTLAND   Did you go on the stage as an amateur?

ALLEN   Yes. The audiences used to throw things at the amateurs. One night a man threw three eggs and a railroad ticket at me. I picked up the railroad ticket and left Boston.

PORTLAND   Were you gone long?

ALLEN   Twenty years. For twenty years my mother kept a light burning in the window for me. When I came home my mother gave me a royal welcome and a gas bill for $729. But enough about me: what's in the news?

PORTLAND   The Fish and Wildlife Service says the big-game population of the country is up 25 per cent.

ALLEN   Say, if big game keeps increasing, someday there will be more animals than people. If the animals learn how to vote, a moose can become President.

PORTLAND   If the animals took over, would people become extinct?

ALLEN   It's possible. The animals might keep a few people in the Zoo. Elks would run around wearing human teeth.

PORTLAND   If people become extinct, what will it be like?

ALLEN   It will be like Philadelphia on a Sunday.

Or:

ALLEN   Pull up a platitude, Portland, and sit down. What is your opening proclamation?

[166]

PORTLAND   In England the House of Commons wants better English coffee for American tourists.

ALLEN   It's about time. When I was in London I tried some of that English coffee. It looked like dirty Mercurochrome. Some of the coffee spilled on my hand and cured a cut on my thumb.

PORTLAND   The paper said that in a British restaurant some tea sold as coffee was thought to be cocoa.

ALLEN   That is possible. English coffee tastes like water that has been squeezed out of a wet sleeve. A corduroy sleeve with a patch on it. Well, what else is new?

PORTLAND   The Easter parade. It was wonderful.

ALLEN   I saw two termites following a guy with a walking stick.

PORTLAND   Forty live mink were marching in the parade, doing stunts.

ALLEN   Forty live mink doing stunts?

PORTLAND   When they got to Forty-second Street the mink spelled out "I. J. Fox."

ALLEN   Fine. Anything else?

PORTLAND   Australia sent three platypuses to the Bronx Zoo.

ALLEN   Yes. I hear the Bronx is returning the favor and sending three people from the Bronx over to the Australian zoo.

PORTLAND   What is the platypus like?

ALLEN   It's small. It has fur. It looks like a possum whose nose has been stepped on. The platypus has been on earth fifty million years.

PORTLAND   Gosh. There sure are some strange things walking the earth.

ALLEN   Yes. Have you ever seen the studio audience coming out after We, the People finishes?

PORTLAND   I mean birds and animals.

ALLEN   Have you ever heard of the chinchilla-winged siskin?

PORTLAND   What is the chinchilla-winged siskin?

ALLEN   It's a tropical bird. It bites people to death and feeds on their screams.

PORTLAND   Gosh!

ALLEN   Do you know the four-toed gecko?

PORTLAND   The four-toed gecko?

ALLEN   The four-toed gecko is a jungle swine. It chases people out into the sun and eats their shadows. But enough of this, Portland. Let's move along to Allen's Alley. . . .

That popular breakfast food that is "shot out of guns" used to remind me of our new dialogue. The lines looked as though they had been written with a riveting machine dipped in ink. The guest star had to be crammed into a ten-minute period. In the ten minutes we had to have a plot that let the audience meet the guest under some unusual circumstance. Somehow that either led into a comedy scene or a reason for the guest to foal a specialty.

Instead of boring you by trying to explain the vague mechanism of this technique, you will probably enjoy examining it yourself. For your pleasure and edification here is a script written for Doc Rockwell on one of our early shows.

Rockwell Hillbilly Skit

ALLEN   Doc, what are you doing buying legal books? The last time I saw you, you were a doctor.

ROCKWELL   I'm a lawyer now, Fred. I've got my own law firm up in Maine.

ALLEN   But Doc, what do you know about law?

ROCK   I studied, Fred. I went to law school at night. When I graduated they gave me a degree and a neon diploma.

ALLEN   What law school did you go to?

ROCK   The University of Maine. I graduated *magna cum lobster.*

ALLEN   At the University of Maine?

ROCK   Yes, I'm the first student they've had since Rudy Vallee.

ALLEN   And you really learned law?

ROCK   Learned law? The day I graduated I sued the college, won the case, and got my tuition back. But law is a fascinating profession, Fred. I had a case last week: *Falvey Harkins* VERSUS *Mona Pruitt.*

ALLEN   What happened?

ROCK   Well, this Mona Pruitt bought a new electric blanket. The first night she slept under the blanket Mona woke up and found a man prying open her window. It was my client Harkins. She had him arrested for burglary. But thanks to me Harkins had an air-tight alibi.

ALLEN   What alibi?

ROCK   I knew Mona had an electric blanket so I claimed that Harkins was trying to get in to read her meter.

ALLEN   Through a window?

ROCK   I proved Harkins was allergic to doors. If he touched a door he broke out in knobs.

ALLEN   Fine.

ROCK   The other lawyer tried to trip me. He asked me how Harkins could read Mona's meter in the dark. I claimed that Harkins had a seeing-eye owl. Harkins had feathers on his sleeve — the rest was routine.

ALLEN   Doc, I'd like to see you in court some time trying one of these cases.

ROCK   You have to know all the tricks, Fred. Last week I had a case up in Maine. Here's what happened. Just as I came in the courthouse . . .

MUSIC   *"Chicken Reel"*

ROCK   Rise, rubes! His honor, Judge Allen!

ALL   Hi, Jedge!

ALLEN   Hi, rubes! *(Raps gavel)* Court's open! Phew! What's that smokin'? That you, Lawyer Rockwell?

ROCK   Yes, Judge. I've got a fire in my briefcase.

ALLEN   Creepers! Smells like somebody's givin' a mummy a hotfoot. Tromp her out.

ROCK   I can't, Judge. I'm trying an arson case tomorrow. I've got to keep this blaze going. It's evidence.

[170]

ALLEN   Well, bank yer briefcase, or suthin'. Fust case, *Town of Possum Pond* VERSUS *Welby Tidball*. And the charge is — Murder! Welby Tidball to the bar.

WELBY   Nobody's bowlin' with my ball, Jedge.

ALLEN   Charge says ye shot unto the death the waitress at the Eagle Hotel — to wit, Sonia Snide. Guilty or not guilty?

WELBY   If I tell ye now I'll spoil the trial.

ALLEN   Okee, Welby. Stand down. Prosecution ready?

ROCK   Yes Judge. I'll call my first witness. Fenton Frisby to the bar.

FRISBY   Comin', comin'.

ROCK   Now, Fenton —

FRISBY   Talk loud. There's a slow leak in my ear trumpet. Other noises keep seepin' in.

ROCK   What is your occupation, Fenton?

FRISBY   I'm the owner, room clerk, house detective and bell boy at the Eagle Hotel. Rooms, seventy-five cents. With fly swatter, a dollar.

ALLEN   No baths?

FRISBY   Rooms with a hose is extra.

ROCK   Fenton, did you know Sonia Snide?

FRISBY   Sonia was my head waitress at the hotel. When Sonia'd start bringin' flapjacks in for breakfast, she'd look like a walkin' jukebox.

ROCK   Fenton, tell the court what happened on the morning of the murder.

FRISBY   I was in the kitchen, fryin' a dove.

ALLEN	Ain't nothin' sweeter than dove meat.
FRISBY	I like a cut right up under the wing.
ALLEN	I like the part of the dove — on a boat, it'd be the rudder.
ROCK	Gentlemen, this isn't a cooking class. This is a murder trial. Now, Fenton, what happened?
FRISBY	I had my ear trumpet down in the pan to see if the dove was fryin'. I looked up. Welby Tidball was comin' in the hotel.
ROCK	Did Welby look mad?
FRISBY	He was carryin' a gun and talkin' to hisself.
ALLEN	What was he sayin'?
FRISBY	Sounded like a man's name. Tommy or Johnny.
ROCK	Couldn't you hear?
FRISBY	My ear trumpet was in the fryin' pan, waitin' for the dove to sizzle.
ROCK	What did Welby do?
FRISBY	He run upstairs. When he come back down his gun was smokin'. I called the Sheriff. There's a "No Smokin'" sign in the lobby.
ROCK	Nice work, Fenton.
ALLEN	Stand down!
	(Gavel raps)
ALLEN	Who's next, Rockwell?
ROCK	Sheriff Pruett to the bar.
SHERIFF	Make way for the law! Stand back, I'm spinnin' my billy!
ROCK	Sheriff, where were you when Fenton called?
SHERIFF	I was out trackin' down Communists.

[172]

ALLEN   Trackin' down Communists?

SHERIFF   There was a man with a sickle, Jedge. I musta followed him fer three hours.

ROCK   A man with a sickle?

SHERIFF   I was waitin' for him to pick up a hammer. I was gonna pounce.

ALLEN   Never mind yer cold war, Sheriff. What about this murder?

ROCK   The judge is right, Sheriff. Stop throwing your billy up in the air and stick to the facts.

SHERIFF   Well, I was on my way to the bus depot, lookin' fer Feller Travelers, when I heared Fenton in the door of the Eagle Hotel yellin' "Murder."

ROCK   What did you do?

SHERIFF   I spit on my badge. Took a tight hold on my billy and ran into the hotel. Fenton took me up to Sonia's room. And there she was.

ROCK   Dead?

SHERIFF   A corpus delicious.

ALLEN   Jeepers!

SHERIFF   Sonia'd been fixin' her hair, Jedge. She was shot plum through the lanolin.

WELBY   She had it comin', Jedge.

                    (Gavel raps)

ALLEN   Quiet, Welby. Hush yer fuss. Proceed, Rockwell.

ROCK   Did you find any clues in Sonia's room, Sheriff?

SHERIFF   Only one. There was a briefcase.

ALLEN   A briefcase? Whose briefcase was it?

SHERIFF   Lawyer Rockwell's.

ALLEN   Lawyer Rockwell's? Stand down, Sheriff.

SHERIFF   Oke bebe dokey, Jedge.

(Gavel raps)

ALLEN   Lawyer Rockwell to the bar.

ROCK   Your honor, I can explain everything.

ALLEN   If ye don't ye'll end up sendin' yerself to the chair.

ROCK   Give me a chance, Judge. I'll cross-examine myself.

ALLEN   You ain't tamperin' with no witness, Rockwell. What was your briefcase doin' in Sonia's room?

ROCK   I saw Sonia the night before about her divorce.

ALLEN   Sonia was married?

ROCK   Yes. After the war she started corresponding with a soldier in Tokio.

ALLEN   Ayar.

ROCK   After a few letters they decided to get married.

ALLEN   Ayar.

ROCK   The soldier couldn't get home so they decided to marry by telephone.

ALLEN   Ayar.

ROCK   The telephone operator was an old maid. Hearing it was a wedding she got nervous and gave Sonia the wrong number in Tokio.

ALLEN   Sonia married a wrong number?

ROCK   Later she found out her husband was Japanese.

[174]

ALLEN   Well, I swan to pucker.

ROCK   Sonia's divorce just came through, signed by General MacArthur. I took it up to her, plus the four dollars the telephone company refunded.

ALLEN   You can prove, Rockwell, these are the facts as as so-stated?

ROCK   Her sister Millie was in the room all the time, Judge. You can ask her.

(Gavel sounds)

ALLEN   Is Millie Snide in court?

MILLIE   Ayar, Jedge.

ALLEN   Step to the bar, Millie. Where are ye?

MILLIE   I'm all in black. I'll raise my veil a mite so's you kin see me.

ALLEN   You're the sister of the departed?

MILLIE   I'm wearin' her shoes, Jedge.

ALLEN   The night of this briefcase episode. Was lawyer Rockwell sweet-talkin' Sonia?

MILLIE   No, Jedge. Sonia was fixin' to marry Welby Tidball.

WELBY   She was a two-timin' Jezebel!

(Gavel raps)

ALLEN   Order! Welby, if you wasn't the defendant, I'd bunt you outta court. Proceed, Rockwell.

ROCK   Millie, when did your sister first fall for Welby?

MILLIE   Welby come into the hotel dinin' room wearin' a raccoon smock and carryin' a paintbrush and road map.

ALLEN   A paintbrush and road map?

[175]

MILLIE   He was a Burma-Shave poet, Jedge. Sonia was a dactyl in his hands.

ROCK   It was love at first sight?

MILLIE   Their eyes met over a bean tansey.

ALLEN   Welby start sparkin'?

MILLIE   When the soup wasn't too hot Welby'd put his hand in and hold Sonia's thumb.

ALLEN   He was givin' her the old rinky dink, eh?

MILLIE   After every meal Welby'd leave Sonia a poem.

ROCK   He'd leave a poem?

MILLIE   Instead of a tip. One poem went:

> *Cute as a butterball — red as a beet*
> *Me for you, Sonia — when can we meet?*

ROCK   Yes?

MILLIE   And then he wrote:

> *Bacon crisp and eggs once over,*
> *Marry me and we'll be in clover.*

ALLEN   I hope his intentions was better than his rhymin'.

MILLIE   The weddin' was set for the mornin' he killed her.

ROCK   What happened that morning, Millie?

MILLIE   Well, Sonia was doin' her hair and I was leavin' for the A and P to get some rice.

ROCK   Yes?

MILLIE   The phone rang. It was Welby. I called Sonia to the phone and went to the store.

ROCK   And when you returned?

MILLIE   Sonia was dead. The weddin' was off. And I had boiled rice for dinner.

ALLEN   Step down, Millie.

[176   ]

MILLIE   Thankee, Jedge. I'm droppin' my veil.

ALLEN   Where'd she go?

MILLIE   Here I be, Jedge. Peek-a-boo.
                    (Gavel sounds)

ALLEN   Next witness.

ROCK   Welby Tidball to the bar.

WELBY   I seen the streak of her bacon, Jedge. I made her
           yell Euchre.

ALLEN   Court'll decide.

ROCK   Welby, is it true you were in love with Sonia
           Snide?

WELBY   To me, Sonia was prettier than a peacock backin'
           into a sunset. I used to dig up the ground she
           walked on and take it home.

ALLEN   That was love.

WELBY   Every night I'd bring Sonia a poke of sweets.
           Then I'd stay in her front yard till all hours skin-
           nin' the cat.

ALLEN   In my book — that's courtin'.

ROCK   When did your feelings change towards Sonia?

WELBY   The first time she mentioned that other man.

ROCK   What other man?

WELBY   Tony somebody.

ROCK   Tony?

WELBY   Every time we had a date — Tony always came
           first.

ALLEN   Ayar.

WELBY   I thought she was givin' me the hard to get, Jedge.
           So I proposed.

ALLEN	And?
WELBY	Sonia accepted.
ALLEN	Ayar.
WELBY	I was lark-happy. I bought a corduroy dickey and two tickets for Niagara Falls.
ROCK	What changed your mind, Welby?
WELBY	Well, the weddin' was set for noon. I called up. I says, "Sonia, are you ready?" She says, "Welby, you'll have to wait."
ROCK	Wait for what?
WELBY	I says, "What's holdin' you up?" She says, "My Tony."
ALLEN	Tony again, eh?
WELBY	On my weddin' day. It was the last straw, Jedge. I took ma gun and went over and made myself a widower.
ALLEN	Looks like justifiable homicide to me.
ROCK	Your honor, I'll prove it wasn't justifiable.
ALLEN	But another man had his straw in Welby's soda.
ROCK	Judge, there was no other man.
ALLEN	No other man?
ROCK	Look at this picture of the deceased.
ALLEN	Ayar?
ROCK	Now look at her sister, Millie.
ALLEN	I'll be hoo-danged. They're twins!
MILLIE	That's right, Jedge. We're the Toni twins.
ALLEN	The Toni twins!
MILLIE	I've got the fifteen-dollar permanent.
ROCK	And Sonia had the Toni permanent.

ALLEN   You mean every time Sonia mentioned Toni —

ROCK   She was fixing her hair. What do you say to that, your honor?

ALLEN   Justifiable homicide.

ROCK   What?

ALLEN   It may not have been a man, but Toni went to her head.

WELBY   And I blew her top, Jedge.
            (Gavel sounds)

ALLEN   Case dismissed! Court adjourned!

Allen's Alley was the most successful comedy device we ever employed during our eighteen years in radio. The Alley was opened officially as a laughing lane on December 13, 1942. The idea had been bobbing around in my mind for many years. The late O. O. McIntyre was indirectly responsible for the Alley. Mr. McIntyre wrote a popular newspaper column in that era and occasionally he ran a feature called "Thoughts while Strolling." O. O. never left his hotel room, but he would describe the sights he saw and the people he met strolling through the shabby streets of Chinatown and the Bowery. I felt that something of this type which would permit me to stroll through a nondescript neighborhood and discuss current events with its denizens would be very amusing. I knew that with music and sound effects we could establish the locale and that it would come off well in radio.

For the first few half-hour shows we used the news-reel idea. I knew the Alley would require a permanent cast and I

[179   ]

knew that the radio audience soon tired of the same comedy characters every week. I also knew that we had been on a long time and I suspected that anonymity could be monotonous, too. It might be a novelty for the audience if we developed several characters they could associate with our show.

A loud-mouthed politician seemed to have possibilities. With the right voice the character would have color in radio. The Senator could give his opinions of the people in government and advise them on how things should be run down in Washington. We had a talented actor in our stock company named Jack Smart. Jack, a buxom-type fellow, became Senator Bloat. The Senator was available for argument on any side of any argument and his solution always was "I will pass my Bloat Bill!" The Bloat Bill would settle the national debt, save the OPA, get socialized medicine going. The Senator promised bifocal contact lenses to old people with short arms who couldn't reach up and put on the old-fashioned glasses. Senator Bloat stayed in office for two years. Then Jack Smart went out to California to become an orange, or something, and Senator Bloat disappeared from Allen's Alley and the national scene.

John Doe was another early Alley character. John Doe, played by John Brown, was the average man. Doe was always incensed about forces and people who were hampering his survival. Brother Doe always had a chip on his shoulder that he was ready to use to kindle an argument. As soon as John Doe had his say he would slam the door in my face and leave me standing forlornly in the Alley.

At the start, these were the only two Alley residents who

were typed. For some time, Charlie Cantor did a stooge character named Socrates Mulligan. Socrates had no political point of view or any established traits. He was just a jolly cretin. At school Socrates' report card showed that he flunked in recess and got a D in lunch. If he is rampant today Socrates is probably sitting with a friend in some dilapidated lunchroom with two plates of alphabet soup before them engaged in a messy game of wet Scrabble. Socrates Mulligan finally moved out of Allen's Alley and, using the name of Clifton Finnegan, enjoyed many years of acclaim flaunting his ignorance about the mildewed premises of Duffy's Tavern.

For the next three years tenants came and went in Allen's Alley. We still had Falstaff Openshaw, the poet, played by Alan Reed, who was very popular for a time. We had a Greek restaurant owner and philosopher; an Italian; an old maid; a gentleman who always came to the door intoxicated. He always thought he was in the street and I was in the house. We had a little boy who would never call his mother; a Russian named Sergei Strogonoff. The Russian was quickly dropped. A man named Sergei Strogonoff threatened to sue. I thought I had invented the name: Strogonoff is a Russian beef dish prepared with milk; Sergei is a common Russian name. When Sergei Strogonoff showed up I didn't argue. After Sinbad Brittle accosted me in Biddeford, Maine, you can tell me your name is Ossip Knothole. I will believe you.

Finally, after three years of experimentation, we found a set of tenants who were to bring Allen's Alley the fame this insane cul-de-sac was to enjoy as long as the program was to endure. During this regime, if you walked down Allen's Alley and looked up at the nameplates on the houses you were passing you would realize that these were the homes of Senator Claghorn, Titus Moody, Mrs. Nussbaum and Ajax Cassidy.

Every Sunday night, when the radio audience walked down Allen's Alley with me, this is a sample of what they heard:

Allen's Alley

PORTLAND	What is your question tonight?
ALLEN	Well, recently license commissioners around the country have been investigating unscrupulous used car dealers and others who have been forcing accessories on automobile buyers. And so our question is: "Have you had any unusual experience trying to buy a new car?"
PORTLAND	Shall we go?
ALLEN	As the little boy's lips said to the bubble gum — the time has come to blow.
	(Allen's Alley theme music)
ALLEN	What a night in Allen's Alley, Portland. I guess the Senator's cooking dinner. I can smell the Yamburgers from here. Let's knock.
	(Knock on door, door opens)
SENATOR	Somebody — Ah say somebody — somebody whammed mah what's-this.
ALLEN	Yes, I —

SENATOR	Claghorn's the name. Senator Claghorn, that is.
ALLEN	Look—
SENATOR	Son, why don't you go away? Go button your nose. Go hem a hanky, son.
ALLEN	I'm sorry, Senator. If you're busy—
SENATOR	Ah jest come back from mah college Alma Mammy. They gimme a degree.
ALLEN	A degree—for what?
SENATOR	Research. Ah wrote a paper on Horace Greeley. Ah proved he was cross-eyed.
ALLEN	Horace Greeley cross-eyed?
SENATOR	Ah proved when Horace Greeley said "Go West"—
ALLEN	Yes?
SENATOR	He was lookin' South.
ALLEN	You must have had some Commencement Day.
SENATOR	They gimme a muleskin diploma and mah degree. What a sight! The entire faculty of Yazoo Normal standin' there—me wearin' mah mortarboard and seersucker robe. When Ah finished mah talk on "Is the Magnolia Doomed?" the student body rose and gimme three cheers and a possum.
ALLEN	It must have been touching. But tell me, Senator, what about this used car business?
SENATOR	Ah hit the ceilin', Son. But it didn't help. Ah had to pay over the ceilin'.

ALLEN | What happened?

SENATOR | Ah went to a used car dealer: the Chucklin' Confederate.

ALLEN | I see.

SENATOR | Ah had mah name on a list four years. Finally the Chucklin' Confederate sent word mah car had come. He said along with the car I'd have to take some accessories.

ALLEN | Accessories?

SENATOR | There was linsey-woolsey seat covers, a weevil spray, swamp pontoons, a built-in hall tree, a canvas hammock, a sundial, a melodeon, two fly-swatters, and a set of musical jugs for a horn.

ALLEN | I see.

SENATOR | Ah was willin' to pay the swindle. Ah had mah shoe off countin' out the money.

ALLEN | Uh-huh.

SENATOR | Somethin' told me to take a gaze under them accessories.

ALLEN | You did?

SENATOR | Ah folded mah money, put mah shoe back on, ah called that Chucklin' Confederate a buzzard's whelp, and stalked outta that junk-yard.

ALLEN | After waiting four years for a car you didn't take it? Why not?

SENATOR | Son, the car was a LINCOLN! So long, son! So long, that is!

[184]

(Door slams)

ALLEN   Well, the Senator solved his problem. I hope we catch Mr. Moody before he dozes off.

(Knock on door, door opens)

TITUS   Howdy, Bub.

ALLEN   You look depressed, Mr. Moody. Is something wrong?

TITUS   My wife lost an ear.

ALLEN   Your wife lost an ear? In an accident?

TITUS   She was carryin' a basket of corn in from the barn.

ALLEN   And?

TITUS   My wife lost an ear.

ALLEN   Fine. Tell me, Mr. Moody, have you had any experience buying a car recently?

TITUS   I was rooked to a fare-thee-well. I was trimmed nearer than a floor-walker's mustache.

ALLEN   No kidding?

TITUS   Effen I ain't a rube, I'll do till one gits here.

ALLEN   What happened?

TITUS   Well, 'bout two months ago I sold my collection of wishbones.

ALLEN   You collected wishbones?

TITUS   I had all kinds of wishbones. Mouse wishbones, rabbit wishbones, ferret wishbones.

I had a horse's wishbone. 'Twas nine feet long.

ALLEN   And you sold your wishbone collection?

TITUS   I was plannin' to buy a car. I sewed my money into one of my mittens and jumped a Greyhound Bus for New York.

ALLEN   What about the car?

TITUS   I was winder-shoppin' around, sizin' things up. I was lookin' in a winder on Broadway. Somehow a stranger standin' next to me got his thumb caught in the buttonhole of my lapel.

ALLEN   I see.

TITUS   Next thing I knowed he was pullin' me into a doorway.

ALLEN   What did this stranger want?

TITUS   At first I thought he was lonesome and jest wanted company. Then he says, "Fixin' to buy a car, Reuben?"

ALLEN   Uh-huh.

TITUS   I says, "What's it to ye?" He says, "Don't git in a pucker. I'm yer man."

ALLEN   The stranger was a car salesman?

TITUS   He took me over to the river. There was a big yard. 'Twas full of fenders, bumpers, engines, bodies and all kinds of parts. I says, "What's this?" He says, "It's a car cafeteria."

ALLEN   A car cafeteria?

TITUS   He says, "You tell me what kind of a car ye

	want. I'll go into the yard and assemble the pieces. But 'fore I start makin' yer car to order," he says, "you kin pay me the money."
ALLEN	Uh-huh.
TITUS	I shook out my mitten. He puts the money in his pocket. He handed me an automobile horn. He says, "Hold this horn, Hayseed. I'll git the rest of yer car together." With that he walked into the yard.
ALLEN	What happened?
TITUS	I was there holdin' the horn. The stranger never come back.
ALLEN	Didn't you tell the police?
TITUS	Long 'bout midnight a constable come by. I told him about the automobile. I showed him the horn the stranger gimme. I was wastin' my time.
ALLEN	The policeman didn't give you any satisfaction?
TITUS	He says, "You got the horn, ain't ye?" I says, "Yes, I got the horn."
ALLEN	Uh-huh.
TITUS	He says, "Well, blow, Brother!" So long, Bub!
	(Door slams)
ALLEN	Titus is like medicine. He's always being taken. Let's try this next door.
	(Door knock, door opens)
MRS. NUSSBAUM	Howdy doody!

[187]

ALLEN	Ah, Mrs. Nussbaum. That's a pretty gown you have on.
MRS. N.	It is mine cocktail dress.
ALLEN	I didn't know you went to cocktail parties.
MRS. N.	We are only living once. *N'est-ce pas?*
ALLEN	That is true.
MRS. N.	Why not enjoining? *C'est la vie.* Life is a deep breath. You are exhaling, it is gone.
ALLEN	How true. I didn't know you were given to tippling.
MRS. N.	Tippling. I am reading everything Tippling is writing. Boots, Fuzzy Wuzzy, Gunga's Din.
ALLEN	No no. Tippling is drinking.
MRS. N.	I am drinking only cherry soda — Dr. Brown's — with occasionally a Catskill Manhattan.
ALLEN	What is a Catskill Manhattan?
MRS. N.	A glass beet soup with inside floating a small boiled potato.
ALLEN	I hate to break this up, Mrs. Nussbaum, but have you had any experience buying a car?
MRS. N.	Pierre, mine husband, is buying secondhand.
ALLEN	Really? What car did you finally buy?
MRS. N.	Pierre, without the glasses, is going to a friend, Pincus, a used-car baron.
ALLEN	Pierre bought a car without his glasses?
MRS. N.	He is bringing home a limousine. It is long and black.

[188]

ALLEN	Fine.
MRS. N.	All around four sides is windows — glass. Hanging down inside is black drapes with also tassels.
ALLEN	Black drapes?
MRS. N.	On the sides is silver lamps. It is riding six people.
ALLEN	Six people?
MRS. N.	While one is outside driving —
ALLEN	Yes?
MRS. N.	Inside, on the floor, is laying five.
ALLEN	This isn't a limousine. It's a hearse.
MRS. N.	This I am telling Pierre.
ALLEN	You refused to ride in it?
MRS. N.	I am saying, "Pierre, darling, foist you are doing one thing and I am riding!"
ALLEN	Before you would ride in the hearse with Pierre, what did you tell him to do?
MRS. N.	Drop dead! Dank you!

(Door slams)

ALLEN	And that brings us to Mr. Cassidy's shanty. I wonder what is happening Chez Cassidy tonight?

(Knock on door. Door opens)

AJAX	What's all the fiddle-faddle? Who's instigatin' the din? Oh . . . How do ye do?
ALLEN	Well, Mr. Cassidy. How are you tonight?
AJAX	Terrible, terrible, terrible. Me right leg is so heavy I can't lift it up.

ALLEN	Your right leg is heavy?
AJAX	It's full of iron. Pig iron.
ALLEN	That's silly. How could your system get full of pig iron?
AJAX	I've been eatin' pork chops. *(Coughs)* I'm not long for this world.
ALLEN	What is that ladder you have there?
AJAX	I'm going over to Sweeney's for dinner.
ALLEN	And you have to carry a ladder?
AJAX	The dinin' room table is too high. You can't sit on chairs. Everybody eats on a ladder.
ALLEN	Why is the dining room table so high?
AJAX	Sweeney is a mounted cop. He always rides in to dinner on his horse.
ALLEN	Oh!
AJAX	Sweeney never uses a napkin. He wipes his hands on the back of his horse. There's so much food on the back of Sweeney's horse, he has mice under his saddle.
ALLEN	Fine. Well, tell me, Mr. Cassidy, what about this used car dealer business?
AJAX	We're livin' in an age of high pressure. People are hounded into buyin' cars with slogans. There's a Ford in your future.
ALLEN	I see.
AJAX	Where I'm goin' in the future, a Ford won't help. What I'll need is a fire engine. With an asbestos hose.
ALLEN	Uh-huh.

AJAX	The Pontiac is the Most Beautiful Thing on Wheels!
ALLEN	What's wrong with that?
AJAX	The most beautiful thing on wheels is Maureen O'Hara on a bicycle.
ALLEN	I see your point.
AJAX	Ask the Man who Owns One.
ALLEN	That's Packard.
AJAX	Have you ever tried to talk to a man in a Packard?
ALLEN	No.
AJAX	Ask the Man Who Owns One. He won't even answer you.
ALLEN	Don't you ever use an automobile?
AJAX	After many years of contemplation, during which I have studied the various means of transportation and weighed their merits pro and con, I have arrived at one conclusion.
ALLEN	And what is your conclusion?
AJAX	That it is best for me to restrict me travel to one type of vehicle.
ALLEN	And that is . . . ?
AJAX	The station wagon.
ALLEN	The station wagon?
AJAX	Every Saturday night when they take me away to the station . . .
ALLEN	Yes?
AJAX	They send the wagon. Good-by to ye, boy!

(Door slams)

[191]

If Allen's Alley had been produced in the theater, and you were in the audience, you would have received a program. Opening the program, you would have read:

Cast of Characters

Senator Claghorn	Kenny Delmar
Titus Moody	Parker Fennelly
Mrs. Nussbaum	Minerva Pious
Ajax Cassidy	Peter Donald

Who were these people? What had they done before? Well . . .

Kenny Delmar was a fine dramatic actor who appeared frequently in the Theatre Guild radio productions and in many serious plays. Kenny was also an accomplished dialectician. The Senator Claghorn character was only one of the vocal cartoons culled from his gallery of comedy creations.

Parker Fennelly was one of radio's pioneer character actors. Shortly after Marconi had turned his invention loose Arthur Allen, another rustic delineator, and Parker were convulsing radio set owners as the Stebbins Boys. In later years they enjoyed a long run in Snow Village Sketches. Parker Fennelly, in my estimation, is the finest simulator of New England types we have in radio, the theater, in Hollywood or even in New England.

Minerva Pious was the most accomplished woman dialectician ever to appear in radio. She worked with us for more than fifteen years and I am an authority on Minerva Pious. There is no subtlety or inflection of speech associated with any nationality that Minerva cannot faithfully reproduce. Her Jewish housewife was never the routine, offensive burlesque caricature. Mrs. Nussbaum was a human being, warm, honest, understanding and — "you should pardon the expression" — very funny.

Peter Donald was a well-known after-dinner speaker. For years Peter had been regaling radio audiences with his great variety of dialect stories, starring on Can You Top This? Today, Peter is ever so gainfully employed in television making guest appearances with his dialect impressions and alternating as moderator and informed member on several panel programs.

You can see that the denizens of the Alley were not the rancid set they seemed to be over the air. Their names were proudly listed in radio's *Who's Who*.

In selecting these types we hoped that Allen's Alley would have regional appeal: Claghorn to please the South; Moody the New England States; Mrs. Nussbaum for the metropolitan areas; Ajax for the Irish who had a sense of humor. It developed that there were a few Irish who didn't. The South didn't resent Claghorn; the Senator was invited to speak at many functions down South and a number of streets in abandoned sections were named after him. Nobody resented Titus Moody. Mrs. Nussbaum, too, appeared to be loved by everybody. Ajax Cassidy, however, was a thorn in the pride of a small fulminating Celtic minority. One militant gentleman who wore no other man's choler was always threatening to march an entire chapter of the Ancient Order of Hibernians down from Albany, or some upstate New York community, to Radio City if Ajax was not evicted from the Alley and chased from the industry. Now that Ajax has become extinct I hope that this champion of his race has been able to stop his bile from perking.

Since I wrote all of the Allen's Alley dialogue down through the years, I got to know the characters pretty well. I liked Titus Moody the best. I had more fun writing his lines and trying to invent things for the old boy to do than I had working on the others. Of course, I come from New England. That may account for my attitude toward Mr. Moody.

As you read the Allen's Alley scripts the sentences may seem terse or abrupt. They had to be constructed that way. The entire Alley was allotted five minutes without laughs — that is actual reading time. Each character had one minute and fifteen seconds to dispose of his subject.

You may recall some of the Senator Claghorn, Titus Moody, Mrs. Nussbaum or Ajax Cassidy high lights from your memory book of forgotten laughs. Some may be in these dissertations:

Titus Moody on Psychiatry

ALLEN   Tell me, Mr. Moody, what about this psychiatry business?

TITUS   I don't know how it works with humans, but I had a hen that had a nervous breakdown.

ALLEN   I see.

TITUS   She was havin' dizzy spells and fallin' off the nest. She was seein' spots before her eyes and tryin' to eat her astigmatism. Finally, her beak got soft.

[194]

	When she went to pick up suthin', her beak would bend.
ALLEN	Gosh!
TITUS	Finish was — she had amnesia.
ALLEN	Your hen had amnesia?
TITUS	She stopped layin' eggs — she forgot what she was. She'd walk between the shafts of a wagon, waitin' to be hitched.
ALLEN	Your hen thought she was a horse?
TITUS	One day. Next day she'd be standin' by the pail, waitin' to be milked.
ALLEN	You called the doctor?
TITUS	He brought a psychiatrist. The psychiatrist says, "Moody, yer hen's got delusions. She's blacked out. We gotta bring her back. Make her know she's a hen."
ALLEN	What did the psychiatrist do?
TITUS	He was eatin' worms to remind her.
ALLEN	Uh-huh.
TITUS	He was jumpin' up and settin' on a nest. When he got off the nest he pulled out a billiard ball and showed the hen — like he'd laid an egg. The billiard ball done it. The hen's back layin' an egg every day.
ALLEN	Fine.
TITUS	There's only one thing.
ALLEN	The billiard ball?
TITUS	She won't lay her egg in the nest.
ALLEN	No?

TITUS The hen walks three miles down the road to the poolroom. So long, Bub!

Titus on Hobbies

ALLEN Tell me, Mr. Moody, have you a hobby?

TITUS I been on Hobby Lobby twice. Fust time, I went to New York with 200 pounds of putty. Savin' putty was my hobby.

ALLEN And what did you do on Hobby Lobby?

TITUS I jest spoke my name. Said the putty was mine. The feller who was runnin' the program felt my putty and said "No hard feelin's" and "Thank you, Mr. Moody." The audience stomped and whistled. I picked up my putty and come home.

ALLEN You went on Hobby Lobby again?

TITUS Ayar. I was collectin' birds' nests. At one time I owned every bird's nest in Rockville Center.

ALLEN Gosh!

TITUS If a bird wanted to lay an egg in Rockville Center, it had to come to me.

ALLEN You didn't abuse this power?

TITUS My window was always open to a feathered friend about to —

ALLEN Good. You've had other hobbies since?

TITUS At one time I was collectin' deer-ends.

ALLEN Deer-ends?

TITUS Everybody was mountin' deer-heads. I started col-

[196]

lectin' what was left over. I had twenty deer-ends
mounted on the walls.

ALLEN   Twenty deer-ends?

TITUS   When I opened the door it seemed like I was over-
takin' a herd.

ALLEN   What is your latest hobby?

TITUS   I've give up hobbies.

ALLEN   Why?

TITUS   Last hobby I had was givin' moose calls. One
mornin' at daybreak I went up to the top of a hill.
I put on an old fur coat and a fur cap. I got down
on all fours. I let out a moose call.

ALLEN   What happened?

TITUS   A big she-moose come over the hill, runnin'.

ALLEN   Uh-huh.

TITUS   She nuzzled up to me and started lickin' my fur
cap.

ALLEN   She was in love with you, eh? What did you
do?

TITUS   I got up and explained as best I could.

ALLEN   And?

TITUS   A big tear come in her eye. She turned and walked
away.

ALLEN   And that's why you've given up your hobby of
moose calls?

TITUS   Yep. Somewhere in them hills tonight —

ALLEN   Yes?

TITUS   There's a moose with a broken heart. So long,
Bub!

[197]

Titus on Mayor La Guardia

ALLEN   Well, Mr. Moody, what do you think about Mayor La Guardia leaving office at last?

TITUS   He's been a good mayor. What there is of him.

ALLEN   What kind of work do you think he should go in for?

TITUS   He'd be a good man on a farm, Bub.

ALLEN   How do you mean?

TITUS   He's the only man I know that can milk a cow standin' up.

ALLEN   Tell me, Mr. Moody, do you think the mayor is sorry to go?

TITUS   I know just how he feels, Bub. I used to be mayor in my town.

ALLEN   Oh? You were the La Guardia of your village?

TITUS   I was mayor, but I wasn't no La Guardia.

ALLEN   You mean —

TITUS   After workin' around a farm for thirty years . . .

ALLEN   Yes —

TITUS   I didn't smell like no Little Flower. So long, Bub!

Titus Moody on the Circus

ALLEN   Tell me, Mr. Moody, what feature of the circus did you like best?

MOODY   Shucks, the circus don't mean nothin' to me. My whole family was circus folks.

[198]

ALLEN   Really?

MOODY   They was freaks, mostly. My uncle Geek Moody: he was knowed as Jo-Jo the Dog-faced boy. He used to pose for dog food ads.

ALLEN   I've heard of Jo-Jo.

MOODY   I had a cousin, Choice Moody. Choice was a fire-eater. He called hisself Dr. Blaze.

ALLEN   I see.

MOODY   One night, Dr. Blaze had a touch of indigestion. He hiccupped three bonfires and set fire to a small group of friends.

ALLEN   Gosh!

MOODY   I had another cousin, Lacy Moody. He went under the name of Elasto, the Rubber Man.

ALLEN   A real rubber man?

MOODY   Elasto could shake hand with ye, and while you was still holdin' his hand he'd go into the next room and start takin' off his things. You could either walk into the next room with Elasto's hand, or you could let go and the hand would snap through the door and back up Elasto's sleeve.

ALLEN   What became of Elasto?

MOODY   He took sick in Duluth. They started to take out his appendix.

ALLEN   Uh-huh.

MOODY   The doctor made the incision . . .

ALLEN   And Elasto the Rubber Man?

MOODY   Died of a slow leak!

Titus Moody on the High Price of Soap

ALLEN	Mr. Moody, what about the rise in soap prices?
TITUS	I quit buyin' it. I been tryin' different things.
ALLEN	Really?
TITUS	I heared 'bout that Swan Soap. I got two swans.
ALLEN	Yes?
TITUS	They didn't give nothin' but eggs.
ALLEN	Probably the wrong breed.
TITUS	I tried makin' my own soap. First, I killed a pig and siphoned off the fat. I put in some olive oil. Added some sodium and alkali. Then I boiled the whole mess, cooled it off, and cut it into cakes.
ALLEN	And how is your soap?
TITUS	'Twon't float, 'twon't bubble, 'twon't clean.
ALLEN	No?
TITUS	When you put it in the water — it jest lays there.
ALLEN	It isn't good for much of anything?
TITUS	If you're lonesome in the tub — it's jest good company.
ALLEN	Fine. How are you bathing now?
TITUS	Every Saturday night I pull out the catalogue. I start lookin' at them high prices.
ALLEN	And?
TITUS	I git in a lather.
ALLEN	You're all set, then. What do you think causes the soap rise?
TITUS	'Twarn't nothin' but politics. The Republicans got

elected. The Republicans says to the Democrats: "We'll take over."

ALLEN   Yes?

TITUS   The Democrats says "No soap!" . . . So long, Bub!

Claghorn on the Nation's Health

ALLEN   Tell me, Senator, what about this move to improve the health of the American people?

CLAGHORN   Ah'm all for it, son! Show me a healthy nation and Ah'll show you a nation that ain't sick. You kin quote me on that.

ALLEN   Thanks. You're behind this health movement, then?

CLAGHORN   Son, last year Ah was on a committee. We raised $80,000 for research in lumbago.

ALLEN   Lumbago?

CLAGHORN   They built a big laboratory. They got a rat — shaved all the hair off its back. On a bitter cold day they put the rat out in the rain. The rat got lumbago.

ALLEN   I see.

CLAGHORN   Fifty doctors and fifty chemists started studyin' the rat, workin' day and night. Finally they produced a Lumbago Serum.

ALLEN   And is the serum a success?

CLAGHORN   It won't cure people, son.

ALLEN   No?

CLAGHORN   But if you know a rat who's sufferin' from lumbago, son, you send that rat to me!

[201]

Claghorn on Music

CLAGHORN   Make it snappy, son. Ah've got to high-tail it. Ah've got to shake mah pegs. Ah'm takin' it on the old tantivy.

ALLEN   Leaving town?

CLAGHORN   Ah'm the guest of honor at Carnegie Hall. The Mobile Philharmonic is givin' a concert. The Mobile Philharmonic is the finest musical aggregation in the South.

ALLEN   A big band?

CLAGHORN   400 men. The leader is Arturo Tuscaloosa. Instead of a baton, Arturo conducts with a hoe-handle.

ALLEN   It must be some outfit.

CLAGHORN   It's the only band in the world with a hound-dog choir. Son, when the Mobile Philharmonic does the Barcarolle, you kin hear the barkin' 20 miles away.

ALLEN   How is the woodwind section?

CLAGHORN   Ah never seen so much wood and heard so much wind.

ALLEN   And the string section?

CLAGHORN   They got rope, hemp, and twine. That's string aplenty.

ALLEN   And the brass?

CLAGHORN   They carry thirty spittoons. More brass than that is showin' off.

ALLEN   What numbers does the Mobile Philharmonic play?

CLAGHORN   All the classics, son. Everythin' by Rimsky Cul-
pepper. The Georgia Cracker Suite. The Flight
of the Boll Weevil. Poet and Sharecropper.
Moonshine Sonata. Rhapsody in Grey. And
no concert is complete without the Claghorn
Fifth.

ALLEN   You wrote it, Senator?

CLAGHORN   Ah drink it! Ha! Ha! Ah'm too fast for yer, son.
Admit it. You ain't got it upstairs. Or downstairs
neither!

Claghorn on Washington Politics

ALLEN   Here comes a man down the street wearing bull-
dog Wedgies. Pardon me, sir.

CLAGHORN   Claghorn's the name. Senator Claghorn, that is.
Stand aside, son! Don't hold me up! Ah'm busier
than a flute player's upper lip durin' a rendition
of William Tell.

ALLEN   You're busy?

CLAGHORN   Ah'm checkin' on that Hoover Report.

ALLEN   What *is* that Hoover Report, Senator?

CLAGHORN   Herby made a list of things he forgot to fix when
he was President. He's givin' the list to little old
Harry so's Harry can fix 'em now.

ALLEN   Fine.

CLAGHORN   Herby says the Army and the Navy is wastin'
money. The Army's throwin' money around like
the taxpayer was the enemy. Ah found one item:

[203   ]

the Army spent two billion dollars for fly swatters
to send to Alaska. When the fly swatters got up
there they found there wasn't no flies in
Alaska.

ALLEN   They sent the fly swatters back?

CLAGHORN   Not the Army, son! The Army spent four billion
dollars more to raise flies to ship to Alaska so's
they could use them fly swatters. That's how the
Army works, son!

ALLEN   I see. What else have you been up to, Senator?

CLAGHORN   Me and Harry opened up the baseball season.
Harry threw out the first ball.

ALLEN   Did the President enjoy participating?

CLAGHORN   He sure did. The way things are goin' Harry'll
play ball with anybody. He couldn't wait to throw
that first ball out to the Washington team, son.
It was the first time this year the Senators took
anything from Harry!

ALLEN   Governor Dewey went to the Yankee game.

CLAGHORN   Ah seen his pitcher in the paper, son! At first Ah
didn't recognize Governor Dewey with that mustache. Ah thought it was some man eatin' a
Hershey bar sideways.

ALLEN   I read that Mr. Dewey is going to Europe.

CLAGHORN   He's doin' the smart thing, son!

ALLEN   Going to Europe?

CLAGHORN   Comin' back, Dewey's goin' to enter the country
as an immigrant and start all over!

[204   ]

Claghorn on A Southern Thanksgiving

ALLEN   You spend Thanksgiving with your family, Senator?

CLAGHORN   With mah kin, son. What a day! Mah Pappy goes out into the woods and kills a possum. Then he goes out in the barnyard and kills a turkey. Then Pappy goes out to the still and kills two gallons.

ALLEN   You have a big dinner?

CLAGHORN   Son, when all the food's on, the four legs of the table is kneelin' down.

ALLEN   What is a Southern Thanksgiving dinner like?

CLAGHORN   We start with a Memphis Martini.

ALLEN   A Memphis Martini?

CLAGHORN   That's a tall glass of pure corn liquor with a wad of cotton in it. A boll weevil's ridin' the cotton. After the drinks comes Dixie canapés.

ALLEN   Dixie canapés?

CLAGHORN   That's a slew of porcupines runnin' up and down the table. On the porcupines' quills is stuck shrimps and cheese and sausage.

ALLEN   After this . . .

CLAGHORN   Every guest is served a big shingle. On the shingle is a live catfish and a watermelon.

ALLEN   A live catfish?

CLAGHORN   To kill the catfish you drop the watermelon on it. Then comes alligator chowder. A whole alligator simmerin' in swamp water. Floatin' on top is mud balls for croutons.

[205]

ALLEN   You have turkey?

CLAGHORN   Mock turkey, son. That's a jumbo raccoon stuffed
           with grits and magnolia buds. For dessert thar's
           a heapin' mound of mint sherbet nestin' in a hog
           jowl. When dinner's over we all stand, raise our
           jugs, and give thanks.

ALLEN   Thanks for what?

CLAGHORN   That we wasn't born in the North!

Mrs. Nussbaum on the Telephone

ALLEN   Well, Mrs. N., today the telephone has been with
           us fifty years. What is your reaction to it?

MRS. N.   Thanks to the telephone, today I am Mrs. Pierre
           Nussbaum.

ALLEN   Really?

MRS. N.   When I am a young girl footloose and fancy,
           mine maiden name is Pom Pom Schwartz.
           Also, I am having two sisters: Caress and Gin-
           ger.

ALLEN   Caress Schwartz?

MRS. N.   Also Ginger Schwartz.

ALLEN   Fine.

MRS. N.   Mine sisters are getting married. Caress is marry-
           ing Skippy Cohen.

ALLEN   I see.

MRS. N.   Ginger is marrying Leroy Berkowitz. He is doing
           well, a pickle salesman, specializing in odd lots,
           by appointment.

[206]

ALLEN   And with both of your sisters married . . . ?

MRS. N.   Sam Cupid is passing me by.

ALLEN   You couldn't get a boy friend?

MRS. N.   I am washing everything in Lox. I am brushing with Pepsodent the teeth. I am taking by Arthur Murray dancing lessons. I am also learning magic tricks and using Mum.

ALLEN   And nothing helped?

MRS. N.   I am still a wallflower.

ALLEN   What finally happened?

MRS. N.   One day, mine father, Ziggy Schwartz, is putting in the house a telephone.

ALLEN   I see.

MRS. N.   On Halloween I am sitting home alone bobbing for red beets. Suddenly the phone is ringing — I am saying hello.

ALLEN   Yes?

MRS. N.   A voice is saying, "Cookie, I am loving you. Will you marry me?"

ALLEN   And you?

MRS. N.   Foist I am saying, "Positively!" Later, I am blushing.

ALLEN   And that is why you say . . .

MRS. N.   Thanks to the telephone, today I am Mrs. Pierre Nussbaum.

ALLEN   But why be so grateful to the telephone company?

MRS. N.   They are giving Pierre a wrong number, dank you!

[207]

Mrs. Nussbaum on Medicine

ALLEN   Mrs. Nussbaum, does your husband Pierre use much medicine?

MRS. N.   Medicine couldn't helping Pierre. He is confidentially — a mental.

ALLEN   Pierre is a mental case?

MRS. N.   All day he is sitting — on his head is tied a greasy string.

ALLEN   A greasy string?

MRS. N.   He is thinking he is a salami end. At night around his feet he is tying the greasy string.

ALLEN   Instead of his head, Pierre ties the greasy string around his feet?

MRS. N.   He thinks he is the other end of the salami.

ALLEN   Has he seen a doctor?

MRS. N.   A psychiatral.

ALLEN   A psychiatrist.

MRS. N.   Either way it is twenty dollars. He is saying to Pierre, "You are not a salami end. . . . You are not a salami end. . . ."

ALLEN   And?

MRS. N.   Pierre is saying, "All right, so I am not a salami end. I will be a pot roast."

ALLEN   Did Pierre go to the psychiatrist often?

MRS. N.   Every day. One day he is shaving off his head. He is a boiled potato. The next day he is standing in a long green bag. He is a pickle. Once he is coming home with three friends — they are cold cuts.

[208]

ALLEN   Tsk! Tsk! Tsk!

MRS. N.   Once, with caraway seeds in his hair, Pierre is a pumpernickel.

ALLEN   After Pierre kept going to the psychiatrist as a salami end, a pot roast, a boiled potato and cold cuts — what happened?

MRS. N.   The psychiatral is getting an idea.

ALLEN   An idea, eh?

MRS. N.   He is opening up a delicatessen.

ALLEN   And what became of Pierre.

MRS. N.   He is hanging in the window. . . . Dank you!

Ajax Cassidy on Gold

ALLEN   Tell me, Ajax, how do you feel about the discovery of gold?

AJAX   Whenever I hear the word "gold" I think of the sad case of Long Dan Dolan.

ALLEN   What happened to Long Dan Dolan?

AJAX   One year Long Dan won the Irish Sweepstakes. He took all the money and had gold teeth put in his head. Long Dan had so many gold teeth he looked as though he had just took a bite out of Fort Knox.

ALLEN   His mouth was yellow, eh?

AJAX   When Long Dan smiled it was like a happy sunset.

ALLEN   What was Long Dan's problem?

AJAX   When word circulated that Long Dan had won the Sweepstakes his relatives started comin' around to borrow money.

ALLEN   And Long Dan had all of his money in gold teeth.

AJAX   He did. But Long Dan was soft-hearted. When a
         relative needed money for rent, Long Dan would
         have a gold tooth pulled and pay the rent. If another
         relative needed an operation, Long Dan would have
         a gold bicustard pulled and pay for the operation.
         Long Dan had the teeth but his relatives were puttin'
         the bite on him.

ALLEN   How long did this continue?

AJAX   For two years. Every other week ye'd see Long Dan
         comin' out of the dentist's office handin' a gold tooth
         to a cryin' relative.

ALLEN   And where is he now?

AJAX   Nobody knows.

ALLEN   After having so many gold teeth pulled out, Long
         Dan disappeared completely?

AJAX   Not completely. In Kerrigan's window there's a life-
         sized oil paintin' of Long Dan Dolan. He hasn't a
         tooth in his head.

ALLEN   But why is his picture in Kerrigan's window?

AJAX   Long Dan Dolan is a Man of Extraction! . . . Good-
         by to ye, boy!

Within the hierarchy of the little men there is no man who
can outlittle the minor executive in a large corporation who
treats his authority as he treats a tight suit. In a tight suit he
is afraid to make a move. With his authority the minor executive takes the same precaution. There are thousands of these
negative men huddled in the places where minor executives

conceal themselves in the labyrinths of the big corporations. They use the clam philosophy. If a clam never sticks its head out it is never overtaken by trouble. If a minor executive never commits himself he can never be cited for anything that has gone askew in the business. It was once rumored that fledgling executives walked around their offices backwards so they wouldn't have to face an issue. It was told that a freshman executive was found suffering from malnutrition lying on the floor in front of the elevator. He had been on his way to lunch and couldn't determine whether he should go up or down. He was afraid to make a decision.

We had men of this ilk in radio. The eternal aggravating factor stemmed from the fact that the actors lasted longer in the industry than the executives. There always seemed to be fresh clusters of busy miniature men making new rules to get things on an efficient basis. As soon as the actors had adjusted themselves to this new regime the miniature men were no longer with the organization. A new pack of trivial fellows were loose in the company feeling their executive oats and making new rules to get things on an efficient basis.

Our program seemed to be forever caught in the tidal wave of executives being swept in and out of office. The new brooms in the organization would just make a sweeping decision and there we were standing in the dust. Each week, as soon as we had prepared our comedy script, all heck (the network censor does not acknowledge the existence of hell) would break loose. The process of creation is imposing form on something that has no apparent form. While we had the empty sheets of paper, and the show was nonexistent, the censor, the agency men and the sponsor were as quiet as a small boy banging two pussywillows together in a vacuum. However, the minute that we had imposed form on the nonexistent, the drones became men of action. When the script appeared, jokes had to be deleted, mention of competitive products and networks had to go and political references were banished lest they stir up somebody in Washington. During the war we could not mention the weather in New York City. The network minds claimed that U-boats off of the shore could pick up our radio program. How it would help the enemy if the crew in a U-boat on the bottom of the ocean off of Easthampton acquired the information that it was a rainy day in New York I could never quite understand. There were so many things in those days I could not quite understand, especially about low-level executive thinking.

There was one petty tyrant in the network whose ambition was to become a legend. With our help he finally made it. You probably do not recall the time that our program was cut off the air. At that precise moment you no doubt had your own troubles; but we were cut off. The newspapers highlighted the incident. The tyrant made a vague statement. We retaliated and had midgets picketing the network building carrying signs reading "This network is unfair to the little man." Feeling, as it gained altitude, ran high. Sides were chosen. Some favored the vindictive executive. Others the comedian.

This is the case history of the decision. With a comedy program it was always difficult to time the show exactly. If the audience was enthusiastic the laughter was sustained and the program ran longer. Since there was no way we could anticipate the audience's reaction, until the program was actually on the air, we had to arrive at an approximate timing. For several weeks we had been running over, and the end of the show had been cut off abruptly. We had told a number of jokes about "our show no end" and one week we started the program with the end of the previous show as a public service. This was to enable people to hear the end of the program they had been denied. Apparently we had been irking the despot. For weeks he must have been spinning madly around on his swivel. Finally, one week, as he read the new script, he decided to crush me under an iron memo. He issued a dictum, shouting up through the air-conditioning so that every employee in the organization might hear his words. Unless certain material deriding network officials was deleted from the script he was going to cut our show off the air. We refused to eliminate something we thought harmless. He refused to dilute his disciplinarian pronouncement. If we did the lines, he would cut us off. We did. And he did.

The executive is no longer with the network. I am. If this is justice it is news to him.

These are the shocking lines that provoked the dilemma:

PORTLAND   Why were you cut off last Sunday?

ALLEN   Who knows? The main thing in radio is to come out on time. If people laugh the program is longer. The thing to do is to get a nice dull half-hour. Nobody will laugh or applaud. Then you'll always be right on time, and all of the little ema-

[213   ]

ciated radio executives can dance around their desks in interoffice abandon.

PORTLAND Radio sure is funny.

ALLEN All except the comedy programs. Our program has been cut off so many times the last page of the script is a Band-Aid.

PORTLAND What does NBC do with all the time it saves cutting off the ends of programs?

ALLEN Well, there is a big executive here at NBC. He is the vice-president in charge of "Ah! Ah! You're running too long!" He sits in a little glass closet with his mother-of-pearl gong. When your program runs overtime he thumps his gong with a marshmallow he has tied to the end of a xylophone stick. *Bong!* You're off the air. Then he marks down how much time he's saved.

PORTLAND What does he do with all this time?

ALLEN He adds it all up — ten seconds here, twenty seconds there — and when he has saved up enough seconds, minutes and hours to make two weeks, NBC lets the vice-president use the two weeks of *your* time for *his* vacation.

PORTLAND He's living on borrowed time.

ALLEN And enjoying every minute of it.

Audience insurance was an innovation we brought to radio in 1948. It wasn't a public service. We had our reasons. When Stop the Music made its debut it was an instant success. If you do not remember this quiz show, and it is possible that you do not, Stop the Music was a simple quiz. A vocal or an instrumental selection was started. At a given cue, an iron-lunged announcer shouted "Stop the Music!" The music was accordingly stopped and the announcer rushed to a phone. A contestant whose number had been called was waiting to play the game. If the contestant at home could name the selection that had been stopped he won a large cash prize and a conglomeration of merchandise. The show was the talk of the country.

Thousands of families refused to leave their homes on Sunday nights while the program was on. They were afraid if Stop the Music called they would lose a fortune. Many poor people had telephones installed hoping that they would be called and find themselves wealthy. Actually the contestants who were to be called during the program at night were notified during the afternoon. Millions of listeners, with high hopes, sitting around their radios at home were wasting their time. They would never be called.

Stop the Music was on another network and was our opposition. I thought if we could insure listeners many of them might continue to listen to our show knowing that financially they would be protected.

The insurance was arranged. The next Sunday night, before our show started, this announcement was made:

ANNOUNCER   Ladies and Gentlemen: Stay tuned to the Fred Allen Show! For the next thirty minutes you are guaranteed. If you — any listener in the United

States — are called on the telephone during the next thirty minutes by any give-away radio program, and because you are listening to Fred Allen you miss an opportunity to win a refrigerator, a television set, a new car, or any amount of cash prize, the National Surety Corporation guarantees that Fred Allen will perform his agreement to replace any article of merchandise up to a value of $5000, or reimburse you for any amount of prize money you may have lost, up to $5000. Notice of any claim under this guarantee must be mailed to Mr. Fred Allen, by registered mail, care of the National Broadcasting Company, Radio City, New York, and postmarked no later than midnight, Monday, October 11, 1948. Relax! Enjoy the Fred Allen Program! For the next thirty minutes you are protected under the terms of a guarantee bond covering all valid claims up to a total of $5000!

During the ensuing weeks a number of claims were made. When the Surety Corporation checked them they discovered that several larcenous listeners were trying to take us up the garden path. Other confused set owners thought we were giving away $5000 and wanted to know what they had to do to get the money. A number of letters came in complaining about the quality of prizes people had won on other give-away shows.

One claim did cause us considerable trouble. It came from

a Harvard student who wrote that while listening to our program he was told that his was the lucky telephone number but he had lost the first prize — an automobile. He wanted us to pay him the value of the car or buy him a new car. We wrote him that the claim would be paid as soon as it had been checked. Before we could even investigate it, the college paper had published a piece denouncing our program and implying that "a famous radio actor was fleecing the poor college student." I had to drop everything and write a snide rebuttal to the allegations. When the Security Corporation examined the claim it became obvious that collusion was on the wing. Two college students were having a go at fraud. One student ran sort of a disc jockey show over a college radio station whose broadcasts only reached the university buildings and the dormitories. One Sunday night, when apparently nobody was listening to the college radio, the disc jockey announced a big quiz show. He called his friend, who said he was listening to our program, and advised him that he was sorry but he had lost the first prize — an automobile. It developed later that the first-prize automobile was a used car, owned by the part-time disc jockey.

After my firsthand experiences I dedicated a monograph to this type of radio program:

Give-Aways

Give-away programs are the buzzards of radio.

As buzzards swoop down on carrion so have give-away shows descended on the carcass of radio.

Like buzzards the give-away shows, if left to pursue their scavenging devices, will leave nothing but the picked bones of the last listener lying before his radio set.

Radio started as a medium of entertainment.

The give-away programs have reduced radio to a shoddy gambling device.

The networks that once vied with each other to present the nation's outstanding acting and musical talent are now infested with swarms of hustlers who are only concerned with the gimmick and a fast buck.

All the promoter of the give-away has to give to radio is the motley array of merchandise he has been able to wheedle out of dealers in return for brief mentions on his clambake.

The give-away program cannot help sales. Its sole appeal is to the greed of the listener. The person who regularly tunes in the give-away show has larceny in his heart. He has no interest in the sponsor's commercials or his products. The give-away fan is only concerned with his selfish incentive — to get something for nothing.

The give-away program cannot help the radio audience. Four or five people win prizes — millions of listeners win nothing. At the end of the program the losers are only thirty minutes older and mad at the sponsor, the master of ceremonies and themselves. The lucky (?) winners rarely receive cash. Their prizes are often useless. An old lady of seventy-five, who gets dizzy wearing high heels, wins an airplane. A man who becomes seasick at the sight of whitecaps on two Good Humor men wins a four-week cruise to South America. A housewife with no teeth wins a lifetime supply of dental floss. A small boy wins a six-room bungalow that has been erected on Fifth Avenue. How he is going to get the six-room bungalow from Fifth Avenue to where he lives is left to the small boy. If he brings the bungalow into the house his parents will probably kill him. If an occasional winner is unfortunate enough to win cash he is instantly surrounded by poor relatives, eager to borrow, real estate and insurance salesmen, anxious to help him invest, and the state and Federal tax collectors who cannot wait to inform him what he owes.

The give-away programs cannot help the radio networks.

The millions of listeners who seek entertainment will eventually flee the give-away programs and radio and turn to television, the theater and leapfrog. Radio City, instead of being a house of joy for the masses will become a Monte Carlo for morons.

What is the solution?

If I were king for one day, I would make every program in radio a give-away show; when the studios were filled with the people who encourage these atrocities I would lock the doors. With all of the morons in America trapped, the rest of the population could go about its business.

If the give-away programs prevail, radio's few remaining listeners will get into the spirit of the thing and give away their radios.

P.S. This was written in 1948. It has come to pass.

During the seven years the half-hour program rolled along, with thirty-nine programs each year, we wrote 273 scripts featuring 273 guests: they were stars from opera and the concert field, top names from the Broadway theater and Hollywood, headliners from vaudeville and leading personalities in the world of sport. To try to insure each guest a successful appearance we created jokes and situations to fit his individual talents. We had the guest segment of the show take on the flavor of the star. If Roy Rogers was the guest there were cowboy songs, a Western sketch and a general atmosphere that the audience would associate with Roy. If Robert Benchley was the guest there was a general atmosphere that depended entirely on Mr. Benchley.

Many celebrities, who could demand higher fees on other programs, preferred to appear with us feeling that they would be presented to better advantage. There was only one exception. On one of James Stewart's New York trips my agent wanted to book him on our show. Mr. Stewart told him that he only planned to do one program while he was in New York. It was his favorite show and he was looking forward to appearing on it. We found another guest to replace him that week and Mr. Stewart appeared on It Pays To Be Ignorant, his favorite show.

A number of well-known stars have broken tradition on our program. Lauritz Melchior, the Metropolitan Wagnerian tenor, appeared as a hillbilly and sang "Open Up Them Pearly Gates." Maurice Evans, the eminent Shakespearian actor, sang "Ragtime Cowboy Joe." And on key, I might add. Shirley Booth sang a bootleg version of *Carmen*. Bea Lillie a homemade interpretation of *Rigoletto*. Leo Durocher rendered an unreasonable facsimile of *Pinafore*. Charles Laughton appeared as a weepy clod in a soap opera; Tallulah Bank-head as the wife of an early-morning husband-and-wife act; James and Pam Mason as a British version of this same pair. Helen Traubel did a singing commercial. Alfred Hitchcock starred in a mystery play that even he couldn't solve. Rodgers and Hammerstein were plaintiffs in a riotous court trial. Bing Crosby did a radio industry version of *The Mikado*. If you are in the mood for name-dropping sometime, let me know. There were many more.

Georgie Jessel, Jack Haley and Henry Morgan were on our show many times. Also, Bert Lahr, Bob Hope, Edgar Bergen, Doctor Rockwell and practically all of the practising comedians. The listeners seemed to enjoy radio comedians working with each other.

Our audience always looked forward to our shows with Jack Benny. Jack has done some convulsing shows as our guest. The Benny-Allen feud, started eighteen years ago, still has some life in it. Recently I worked on Jack's television show and the Hollywood audience reacted to the ancient insults in the same way as audiences have for eons. It might have been an ancient audience.

For years people have been asking me if Jack and I are friendly. I don't think that Jack Benny has an enemy in the world. He is the best-liked actor in show business. He is the only comedian I know who dies laughing at all of the other comedians. He is my favorite comedian and I hope to be his friend until he is forty. That will be forever.

After our long radio association it seemed that Jack should be the one to escort me out of the medium. He did.

Jack appeared as our last guest on our farewell program.

We did many shows together, Jack and I, and one of our favorite scripts still seems funny to me. If you have a few minutes and your magnifying glass handy — see if you don't agree.

ALLEN   Well, yesterday afternoon I left home and started up Third Avenue. I stopped to read a sign in a thriftshop window. Suddenly, from a pawnshop next door, I heard —

JACK   *(Plays "Love in Bloom" on violin)*

ALLEN   Gad! There's only one man, besides Rubinoff, who can make a violin sound like that. I've got to see who is in this pawnshop.
                         (Door opens and closes)

JACK   But, Mr. Rappaport, this violin is a simulated Stradivarius.

ALLEN   I thought so. Jack Benny!
                         (Applause)

ALLEN   Jack, what are you doing here in a pawnshop?

JACK   Excuse me, just a minute, Fred.

ALLEN   Sure.

JACK   Look, for the last time, Mr. Rappaport, will you take my violin?

MR. R.   If there is anything I hate it is making decisions. Let me hear it once again.

JACK   Okay. *(Plays "Love in Bloom")*

MR. R.   Something is with the tone. Let *me* play it.

JACK   All right. Here.

[222]

MR. R.   Now we will see. Listen.

(Orchestra violinist plays "Love in Bloom" beautifully)

MR. R.   That's better.

JACK   It's strange, Mr. Rappaport, you're a pawn-broker and you play my violin better than I do.

MR. R.   Why not? The violin has spent more time with me than it has with you.

ALLEN   Jack, you're not hocking your violin?

JACK   No, Fred. I'm just storing it.

ALLEN   Storing it?

JACK   Yes. I leave my violin with Mr. Rappaport every summer. He puts it in a mothproof bag. It's safe with him.

ALLEN   I see.

JACK   You know how a pawnbroker is — he takes an interest in things.

ALLEN   I know.

JACK   Then you'll take it again this summer, Mr. Rappaport?

MR. R.   All right, Mr. Benny. But please, this time just the violin.

JACK   Just the violin?

MR. R.   Yes. All last summer I had that Phil Harris and Dennis Day hanging in my window.

JACK   Oh, yes! Yes! Well, I guess this summer I can squeeze them into my locker at Grand Central. I've got the Quartet in there already.

MR. R.   Any place but here, Mr. Benny. Here's your ticket. I'll put away your violin.

[223   ]

JACK   Thanks a lot. Haven't you forgotten something, Mr. Rappaport?

MR. R.   Oh, yes. Here's a handful of mothballs for your suit.

JACK   Thanks. See you in the fall, Mr. Rappaport. Let's go, Fred.

ALLEN   Okay.

              (Door opens and closes)

ALLEN   Gosh, Jack. You look wonderful.

JACK   And, Fred, you look wonderful, too.

ALLEN   And to think people have been saying you're a shriveled-up, infirm, doddering old man.

JACK   And to think people have been saying you're a flabby, wrinkled, baggy-eyed old sourpuss. They told me you were wearing a veil.

ALLEN   People have been saying that's what we are? Ha! Ha!

JACK   Yes. Ha! Ha! Say, Fred —

ALLEN   Yes, Jack.

JACK   We are, aren't we?

ALLEN   I can't get over it, Jack. I've never seen you looking better.

JACK   Well, thanks.

ALLEN   That beautiful wavy hair —

JACK   Well —

ALLEN   Those sparkling white teeth —

JACK   Gee —

ALLEN   And those long eyelashes —

JACK   Uh-huh. What about my nose?

ALLEN   Your nose?

JACK   Yes. At least that's mine.

ALLEN   No. I mean it, Jack. I don't know how you do it. You look so young.

JACK   Really?

ALLEN   You don't look a day over —

JACK   Over what?

ALLEN   When I'm your age I hope I look as good as you do.

JACK   Now wait a minute, Allen, if you want —

ALLEN   Jack, Jack, what are we arguing for? We're old friends.

JACK   You're right, Fred.

ALLEN   When I told you you were looking good, I meant it. Tell me, Jack, how do you keep yourself in such good condition?

JACK   Well, Fred, it's the life I've been leading. I eat the right food, get plenty of exercise and keep sensible hours.

ALLEN   I see. What's your average day like, Jack?

JACK   Well, I get up every morning at seven, and jump into a cold tub.

ALLEN   A cold tub?

JACK   Yes. Then I fill the tub with hot water, and relax for an hour.

ALLEN   I see.

JACK   Then I'm ready for breakfast. A glass of orange juice and a long loaf of French bread.

ALLEN   A long loaf?

JACK   Yes. I lean on the French bread while I'm drinking the orange juice.

ALLEN   Oh, fine.

JACK   After breakfast I put on a pair of sneakers —

ALLEN   And when you have the sneakers on?

JACK   I sneak back to bed again.

ALLEN   How long do you stay in bed?

JACK   Till lunch. For lunch I eat a health sandwich.

ALLEN   What is a health sandwich?

JACK   One vitamin pill between two wheaties.

ALLEN   Oh. And after lunch?

JACK   I'm off to the golf course.

ALLEN   You play golf?

JACK   If I happen to find a ball, yes. Otherwise, I caddy.

ALLEN   After a hard day of retrieving on the links you must be ready for dinner.

JACK   Yes. For dinner I have two cakes of ironized yeast and a heaping bowl of spinach.

ALLEN   Yeast and spinach. That must give you plenty of iron.

JACK   You said it. I don't know what they do in Rio on a rainy night, but at my house I sit around and get rusty.

ALLEN   Well, Jack, that's some day. No wonder you look in the pink.

JACK   Tell me, Fred, how do *you* keep looking so healthy.

ALLEN   I hang around the Blood Bank all day. At night, when they close up, if they have any blood left over, they give it to me. I'm loaded.

JACK   If I need any plasma I'll know where to come.

ALLEN   You bet. How do you do it, Jack? You haven't a wrinkle in your face.

JACK   Just between you and me, Fred, I have undergone a little plastic surgery.

ALLEN   Plastic surgery?

JACK   Yes. Every so often I have this plastic surgeon take up the slack skin on my face and tie it at the back of my neck.

ALLEN   The back of your neck? Doesn't it bother you?

JACK   No. The only thing is, now I wear a Size 27 collar.

ALLEN   I noticed that your Adam's Apple was pulled around under your left ear. But with it all, Jack, you still look the same as the first day I met you.

JACK   And, Fred, you look the same as the first day I met you.

ALLEN   Remember that first day we met.

VIOLINS   "Memories . . ." *(Sneaks in)*

ALLEN   I was in vaudeville — a star. I was headlining at the Cecil Theater in Mason City, Iowa. After the first show there was a knock on my dressing-room door.

(Knock on door)

ALLEN   Come in!

(Door opens)

[227]

KRAKAUER   Mr. Allen, I'm the manager, Mr. Krakauer. You've got a great act. You're a great star.

ALLEN   Thank you, Mr. Krakauer.

KRAKAUER   With you as the headliner I've got a great show. All but one act.

ALLEN   Oh.

KRAKAUER   I'm canning that guy right now. He's dressing across the hall.

(Knock on door. Door opens)

JACK   Yes?

KRAKAUER   I'm the manager. Your act is putrid. You're canned!

JACK   Everything went wrong. When I came on the orchestra forgot to play "Pony Boy." When I played "Listen to the Mocking Bird" my E-string broke. At the finish when I play "Glow Worm" my violin lights up. The electrician forgot to plug it in.

KRAKAUER   My patrons are Iowa farmers. All week they work in the cornfields. They come to the theater to forget corn, not to have it thrown in their faces. Start packing!

JACK   But Mr. Krakauer —

KRAKAUER   You're through! Get out!

JACK   I wish I was dead.

ALLEN   What's the matter, son?

JACK   The manager canned me.

ALLEN   Come in to my room. Don't hang back, lad.

JACK   But — this is the star's dressing room.

ALLEN   I know.

JACK   You mean you're Fred Allen?

ALLEN   Yes. Stop trembling, son. Sit down.

JACK   Gosh! Me in Fred Allen's dressing room. It's like a dream.

ALLEN   What is your act called?

JACK   Gypsy Jack and his Tzigeuner Fiddle.

ALLEN   Gypsy Jack.

JACK   This is my first date in vaudeville. Now I'm canned.

ALLEN   Don't give up, Gypsy Jack.

JACK   But I haven't any money. I can't get home. I live in Waukegan.

ALLEN   What is the fare to Waukegan?

JACK   Thirty dollars.

ALLEN   Here is thirty dollars, Gypsy Jack. Go back to Waukegan.

JACK   Oh, thank you, Mr. Allen!

VIOLINS   "Memories . . . " *(Fades)*

ALLEN   Gosh, Jack, when I saw you leaving the theater that day in your gypsy suit with the burlap sash, little did I think I would ever see you again. What happened?

JACK   When I finally got home to Waukegan, I went back to pressing pants in my Uncle Tyler's tailor shop.

ALLEN   Mason City had left no scars?

JACK   No. But show business was still in my blood. I used to take my violin around and play for all of my friends.

ALLEN   You were happy.

[229]

JACK   For the nonce. Then, suddenly I had no friends.

ALLEN   And then?

JACK   One day, I was pressing a pair of pants. It was a rush job. The pants belonged to the tenor in a Blossom Time company. They were leaving that night.

ALLEN   I see.

JACK   I was pressing carefully, avoiding the holes, when my iron ran into a lump in one of the pockets. The lump turned out to be a ticket to Hollywood.

ALLEN   Hollywood! That was the second time we met.

VIOLINS   "Memories . . ." *(Fades)*

ALLEN   It was on the 20th Century Fox lot. I was starring in my first picture *Thanks a Million*. I remember that morning I walked on the set . . .

1ST VOICE   Quiet on the Set! Quiet on the set! Mr. Allen is ready for this scene!

2ND VOICE   Here's the script, Mr. Allen.

ALLEN   Thank you.

3RD VOICE   Chair, Mr. Allen?

ALLEN   Thank you.

4TH VOICE   Let me touch up your make-up, Mr. Allen.

ALLEN   Thank you.

RATOFF   Mr. Allen, we are shooting right away the big comedy scene.

ALLEN   Which one, Mr. Ratoff?

RATOFF   It is the Bowery. You do a scene with a bum.

ALLEN	A scene with a bum?
RATOFF	Yes. Joe, bring in the bum.
JOE	This way, you guys! Central Casting sent us fifteen of the seediest extras they could find. Pick out the crumbiest, Mr. Allen.
ALLEN	Hmm. How about that one — in the dirty T-shirt and baggy beret.
JOE	Okay, Hey, you — step forward.
BENNY	Yes, *sir!*
ALLEN	Just a minute, Beaten One. I know your face. Aren't you Gypsy Jack?
JACK	Yes, Mr. Allen. But here in Hollywood my name is Jack Benny.
ALLEN	I hardly knew you with that beard.
JACK	I've been standing-in for Gabby Hayes. This is my big break, Mr. Allen. Gosh, doing a scene with you . . . It's like a dream again.
RATOFF	All right. Let's get going. Cameras ready! Lights!
JOE	Here's the pie, Mr. Allen. *(Hands Fred lemon pie)*
JACK	Wait! A pie?
RATOFF	Yes. It's a very short scene. Mr. Allen hits you in the face with a pie. Camera! Lights! Ready, Mr. Allen.
ALLEN	Ready. *(Gets set to hit Benny)*
JACK	Wait a minute!
RATOFF	Hold it! What is it?
JACK	What do I do?

[231]

RATOFF You do nothing. You just get the pie in the face. Camera! Lights! Get ready to throw, Mr. Allen.

ALLEN I'm ready. (*Gets set*)

JACK One moment, please!

RATOFF HOLD IT! Now what?

JACK Don't I duck or anything?

ALLEN No. You just hold your face still and *Whap* you get it.

JACK It might help if I mug after the *Whap.*

RATOFF Get another bum! This bum is a bum!

ALLEN He'll be all right, Gregory. Now, Jack, pipe down.

JACK Sorry, Mr. Allen.

RATOFF Camera! Lights! Ready, Mr. Allen.

ALLEN All set. (*Gets set*)

JACK Wait a minute!

ALLEN What is it now?

JACK What kind of a pie is it, Mr. Allen?

ALLEN Lemon meringue.

JACK Couldn't they make it banana cream? I like banana cream better.

ALLEN It so happens Mr. Zanuck likes lemon meringue.

JACK Oh!

RATOFF Camera! Lights! Quick, throw it, Mr. Allen!

JACK Hold it! Just one more thing.

RATOFF Now what?

JACK What part of my face is Mr. Allen going to hit? I'd like to get it right so you won't have to

	do the scene over. I'm anxious to make good.
RATOFF	He will hit you between the eyes, so the lemon meringue will drip down on your clothes.
JACK	On my clothes?
RATOFF	We will have them cleaned and pressed for you.
JACK	The pressing I can do myself. I don't want to cause trouble. *(Laugh)*
RATOFF	*(Fast)* Camera! Lights! Quick, Fred!
ALLEN	Okay. *(Gets set)*
JACK	Wait! Wouldn't it be funnier if he hit me with a loaf of bread?
ALLEN	A loaf of bread?
JACK	Sliced.
RATOFF	I've had enough! You're fired! Get off the set!
JACK	But, sir —
RATOFF	That's all for today, everybody! This bum has unnerved me. Put away the pie. *(Fade)* That's all!
ALLEN	Well?
JACK	I wish I was dead.
ALLEN	Look, Gypsy. I told you ten years ago in Mason City —
JACK	But, Mr. Allen, I thought the movies —
ALLEN	Okay, so you don't need talent in movies. You still have to have *something*.
JACK	You're right. I guess I'm just not meant for show business.
ALLEN	Do you still live in Waukegan?

JACK	Yes, Mr. Allen. It's thirty dollars by bus.
ALLEN	Okay. Go back to Waukegan. Here is the thirty dollars.
JACK	Mr. Allen — how will I ever be able to repay your kindness —
VIOLINS	"Memories . . ." *(Sneaks in)*
ALLEN	I'll never forget, Jack, when you left the studio I gave you the lemon meringue pie.
JACK	It lasted me all the way to Green Bay.
ALLEN	What happened when you got back to Waukegan this time?
JACK	I went back to the tailor shop. But my Uncle Tyler wasn't there any more.
ALLEN	There was a new owner?
JACK	And he made life miserable.
ALLEN	He was mean to you?
JACK	All day he kept singing those songs of his from *Blossom Time*. To this day I hate tenors. I hate *Blossom Time*.
ALLEN	You were unhappy, eh?
JACK	I was desperate to get away. Whenever I got a pair of pants to press, the first thing I did was feel for lumps. And then one day —
ALLEN	Another lump?
JACK	A big one.
ALLEN	A railroad ticket?
JACK	This time it was money. I could go where I wanted. I went to New York.
ALLEN	New York. That was the third time we met.

VIOLINS   "Memories . . ." *(Fades)*

ALLEN   New York! That's where you got your start in radio.

JACK   Thanks to you, Fred.

ALLEN   Oh, it was nothing. I remember, that day I got the call from a man named Weaver. A big-shot with the American Tobacco Company. I entered Mr. Weaver's office —

(Door opens and closes)

WEAVER   Gad! Fred Allen! We've been waiting all afternoon.

ALLEN   I got your note, Mr. Weaver.

WEAVER   We've got a big radio program all lined up for Lucky Strike Cigarettes — and we want you to be the star.

ALLEN   I'm sorry.

WEAVER   Wait till you hear this setup — we've got Don Wilson to announce; Rochester, Dennis Day, Phil Harris . . .

ALLEN   But I've just signed to do a program for Tender Leaf Tea and Shefford Cheese.

WEAVER   Well, that does it. Without Allen we might as well pull Lucky Strikes off the market. We'll close the plantations, put LSMFT back in the alphabet, and send old F. E. Boone back to Lexington, Kentucky.

ALLEN   There must be somebody else you can get.

WEAVER   WHO? Singin' Sam wants too much money. The Street Singer went into the real estate busi-

	ness. And what a program we had lined up!
ALLEN	I'm sorry.
WEAVER	We had this quintette hired to do the commercials.
ALLEN	A quintette?
WEAVER	Yeah. Show him, boys!
CAST	HMMMMMMMMMMMMM.
ALLEN	Wait! The guy on the end — aren't you Gypsy Jack?
JACK	Yes, Mr. Allen.
ALLEN	Jack, you in a quintette?
WEAVER	(Sotto) His wife, Mary, is in the show. We did her a favor.
ALLEN	Look, Mr. Weaver, the star of this Lucky Strike show — does he have to be funny?
WEAVER	No. We've got Rochester, Dennis, Phil — plenty of comedians.
ALLEN	Does he have to have any talent?
WEAVER	All we need is a slob the others can bounce jokes off of.
ALLEN	Then here's your man — Jack Benny!
WEAVER	Okay, Benny — you're hired!
JACK	Fred. I'll never — never be able to thank you enough.
VIOLINS	"Memories . . ." (Sneaks in)
ALLEN	So, Jack, that's how you got into radio.
JACK	Yes, Fred, and if it wasn't for the thirty dollars you gave me in Mason City and Hollywood — Say, funny how things slip your mind. I never

did pay you back that sixty dollars. *(Laugh)*

ALLEN No.

JACK I lost your address. And you were traveling around all the time. I tried to find you through *Billboard.*

ALLEN Forget it, Jack.

JACK But it isn't like me.

ALLEN I know. Forget about it.

JACK Gosh, it just happens I haven't got a cent on me right now, or I'd —

ALLEN Please, Jack. Don't mention it again.

JACK I won't. Well, Fred, it's been swell talking over old times.

ALLEN It sure has, Jack. Tell me, what are you doing now?

JACK Nothing. My program finished last Sunday.

ALLEN You're out of work again, eh?

JACK Yes, Fred.

ALLEN What are you going to do?

JACK I guess I'll go back to Waukegan. But, Fred —

ALLEN You don't have to ask me, Jack. Here's the thirty dollars.

JACK But, Fred —

ALLEN And this time stay in Waukegan!

ORCHESTRA "Down in Connachy Square" *(Fade)*

(Applause)

So ends the story of our radio program. Its epitaph reads Born

OCTOBER 23, 1932, AS THE LINIT SHOW — DIED JUNE 26, 1949, AS THE FRED ALLEN SHOW. The program might have enjoyed a few more years on borrowed time but my blood pressure was getting higher than the show's rating and it was a question of which one of us would survive. I did, a mortician friend assures me.

Television was already conducting itself provocatively, trying to get radio to pucker up for the kiss of death. Young men with crew cuts were dragging TV cameras into the studios and crowding the old radio actors out into the halls. Even without the coming of television radio seemed doomed. Year by year the survey figures showed a gradual shrinking in the mass listening audience. The audience and the medium were both getting tired. The same programs, the same comedians, the same commercials — even the sameness was starting to look the same.

Radio was the first free entertainment ever given to the public. Since it was piped into homes it was a service similar to running water. When the novelty of the shows wore off many people had more respect for running water than they did for radio. A house owner who would never think of speaking disrespectfully of the water in his house would rant around his radio set, sounding off about the dubious merits of some program he had just heard.

Radio could not survive because it was a by-product of advertising. Ability, merit and talent were not requirements of writers and actors working in the industry. Audiences had to be attracted, for advertising purposes, at any cost and by any artifice. Standards were gradually lowered. A medium that demands entertainment eighteen hours a day, seven days every week, has to exhaust the conscientious craftsman and performer. Radio was the only profession in which the unfit could survive. When television belatedly found its way into the home, after stopping off too long at the tavern, the advertisers knew they had a more potent force available for their selling purposes. Radio was abandoned like the bones at a barbecue.

Comedy has changed with the coming of television. The radio listener saw nothing: he had to use his imagination. It was possible for each individual to enjoy the same program according to his intellectual level and his mental capacity. In radio, a writer could create any scene that the listener could picture mentally. In television a writer is restricted by the limitations imposed on him by the scenic designers and the carpenter. With the high cost of living and the many problems facing him in the modern world, all the poor man had left was his imagination. Television has taken that away from him.

There was a certain type of imaginative comedy that could be written for, and performed on, only the radio. Television comedy is mostly visual and the most successful of comedians today are disciples of the slapstick. Jack Benny, with his comedy show, has been a star in radio for more than twenty years. I am afraid that twenty years from today none of the current crop of TV comedians will be found cutting their elementary didoes before the cameras.

We are living in the machine age. For the first time in history the comedian has been compelled to supply himself with jokes and comedy material to compete with the machine. Whether he knows it or not, the comedian is on a treadmill to oblivion. When a radio comedian's program is finally finished it slinks down Memory Lane into the limbo of yester-year's happy hours. All that the comedian has to show for his years of work and aggravation is the echo of forgotten laughter.